Chocolate Therapy

Text © 2006 by Kathy Farrell-Kingsley

First published in the USA in 2006 by
Fair Winds Press, a member of
Quayside Publishing Group
33 Commercial Street
Gloucester, MA 01930

10 09 08 07 06   1 2 3 4 5

ISBN 1-59233-178-5

Library of Congress Cataloging-in-Publication Data

Farrell-Kingsley, Kathy.
  Chocolate therapy : indulgent recipes to lift your spirits / Kathy Farrell-Kingsley.
     p. cm.
  Summary: "Recipes using chocolate as the base ingredient"—Provided by publisher.
  ISBN 1-59233-178-5
  1. Cookery (Chocolate) 2. Chocolate—Psychological aspects. I. Title.
  TX767.C5F38 2006
  641.6'374—dc22

                                                              2005024253

Cover design by Mary Ann Smith
Book design by Yee Design

Printed and bound in USA

The information in this book is for educational purposes only. It is not intended to replace
the advice of a physician or medical practitioner. Please see your health care provider
before beginning any new health program.

To Eleanor,   2006.
with all our love
Mum & Dad.

Chocolate Therapy

Indulgent Recipes to Lift Your Spirits

Kathy Farrell-Kingsley

FAIR WINDS
PRESS
GLOUCESTER, MASSACHUSETTS

Contents

Introduction

Why *Chocolate Therapy*?

The desire for chocolate has driven people into the streets at
3:00 in the morning in search of an all-night newsstand that
stocks candy bars. It has led others to do shameful things, like
the woman who showed up at a Godiva store with a perfectly
wrapped gift box of chocolate she had bought the week earlier
for her sister's birthday, explaining that she had figured out
how to get into the box from the bottom and emptied it her-
self. It even has reduced some to trickery, like the man who put
chocolate in the freezer so he wouldn't eat it, only to discover
that it can taste even better frozen.

These are but a few of the true confessions revealed in focus
groups run by Nestlé Chocolate, my former employer. Listening
in on consumers divulging their feelings toward chocolate in
these focus groups was part of my job. I worked as a recipe
developer and national spokesperson for the chocolate divi-
sion, and my workdays were consumed with learning about
chocolate and the chocolate-buying consumer. I studied chocolate with master chocolatiers. I traveled the country demon-
strating chocolate cooking techniques on television and at

festivals and conferences. And I tested and tasted more chocolate recipes than most people could ever imagine. I know an
immense amount about the magical cocoa bean. But what has
always intrigued me most is the emotional and psychological
connection that many of us have with chocolate—and I'm not
ashamed to admit that this includes me.

I take my chocolate seriously. I'm not sure why it is so important to me. But over the years, chocolate has always been there
for me like a friend, never questioning me and always comforting me when I'm down.

This chocolate connection that I share with so many others
is not imagined. Scientists don't know exactly how or why in
many cases, but they do know that chocolate and mood are
unquestionably linked. This relationship is why there's a lineup
every afternoon at the office candy machine; why people eat
more chocolate in the cold, dreary winter months; and why
PMS sufferers can't get enough of the rich, creamy confection.

Chocolate and Well-Being

So where do these chocolate cravings come from? Scientists
have found a compound in chocolate called anadamide that
stimulates brain receptors in a manner similar to that of other
addictive substances. Chocolate cravings may also be triggered
when the taste buds tingle with the taste of chocolate. This
sensation occurs because when chocolate melts on the tongue,
it excites the taste buds. And when the taste buds are excited,
endorphins are released from the brain. These endorphins are
natural opiates, or the body's feel-good chemicals. There are
also certain psychoactive substances in chocolate that can
diminish anxiety, boost a person's sense of well-being, and
trigger feelings similar to those experienced by people falling
in love.

Chocolate as Medicine?

One day, doctors may prescribe a component of chocolate to treat diabetes, stroke, dementia, and even heart disease. After 15 years of research, in 2005, Mars—the maker of such treats as M&Ms and Mars bars—announced plans to develop medications using flavanols, a plant chemical found in cocoa.

Flavanols, which are also found in red wine and green tea, have been shown to improve blood flow. Like aspirin, flavanols thin the blood by reducing platelet aggregation. For the first time, the specific cocoa flavanols responsible for this effect have been identified. "The mounting scientific evidence on cocoa flavanols is extraordinary. This is a scientific breakthrough that could well lead to a medical breakthrough," said Norm Hollenberg, M.D., Ph.D., professor of medicine at Harvard Medical School and one of the first researchers to identify the potential health benefits of cocoa flavanols. Mars is currently in talks with large pharmaceutical companies to potentially develop a major new class of medications based on synthesizing these flavanols.

In two clinical trials, cocoa flavanols were found to increase blood flow to certain key areas of the brain, which means they could potentially be used to treat dementia and strokes. And another clinical study found that the ability of flavanols to improve the synthesis of nitric oxide by blood vessels could be of benefit in treating vascular complications from long-term diabetes.

Although more research is needed before such cocoa-based medications become a reality, the thought of treating serious diseases with a compound found in cocoa is sweet indeed.

There's also plenty of reason to believe that eating chocolate has some health benefits. Chocolate can be very rich in compounds called flavonoids, which can function as antioxidants and help keep the blood from clotting. (For more on the reported health benefits of chocolate compounds, see "Chocolate as Medicine?" on page 9.) Cocoa is unusually rich in two kinds of flavonoids, flavanols and proanthocyanidins, which are especially potent. Studies also show that the flavonoids in chocolate may strengthen the immune system by reducing inflammation. That's important in protecting against heart disease, too, since inflammation of the lining of the artery walls is believed to be part of the damaging process that leads to cardiovascular disease.

And the good news doesn't stop there. Although chocolate contains saturated fat in the form of cocoa butter, most of it comes in the form of stearic acid, which doesn't increase cholesterol levels as much as other saturated fats. Stearic acid is converted in the liver to oleic acid, a heart-healthy monounsaturated fat that can help reduce cholesterol levels.

It isn't surprising that today chocolate is linked to well-being. Almost from the beginning of its use as a food, cocoa has been associated with good health. The Aztec ruler Montezuma is said to have drunk 50 pitchers of chocolate a day to stay strong and healthy. When the Spanish conquistadores arrived in Mexico, one of them called chocolate "the healthiest thing and the greatest sustenance of anything you could drink in the world, because he who drinks a cup of this liquid can go a whole day without anything else."

Cocoa was also believed to help with endurance of another sort, too, as Casanova reportedly consumed it as a prelude to his amorous adventures. Centuries ago it was also prescribed to treat fever, aid digestion, and relieve dysentery. In the seventeenth century it was believed to strengthen the heart—a nod to current findings.

Go for the Good Stuff

In a happy alignment of taste and health, the finest-quality chocolate also turns out to be the best for you. The purest chocolate is composed of three things: cocoa butter, cocoa solids, and sugar. The fats in cocoa butter give chocolate its characteristic texture, since cocoa butter melts at body temperature—the reason why the best chocolate literally melts in your mouth. Cocoa solids give chocolate its complex flavor, and they contain the antioxidants. So it makes sense that the more real cocoa the chocolate contains, the healthier it is.

Some commercially produced chocolate contains added milk fats, hydrogenated vegetable oils (also known as trans fats), emulsifiers, and artificial flavors. To make sure you're buying good-quality chocolate, read the label and choose brands with the highest cocoa content and least sugar and dietary fat. Darker and finer chocolate is 70 percent cocoa; most commercial candy bars are 20 percent. The general rule of thumb is: The darker the chocolate, the better for you.

And that's exactly how I like my chocolate—dark and rich— no wimpy stuff for me. I want it good enough to die for. Every precious bite should permeate my senses and medicate me with its chocolatiness. When chocolate is administered in the right "dose," I know from experience that it can relieve anything from a hard day at the office to a full-fledged existential crisis. When I am stressed, the oozing, bittersweet goodness of a grilled chocolate sandwich unwinds me. When I feel tension building late at night while working at my computer, a steaming cup of rich, creamy chocolate is a sure cure. And, well, do I even need to describe the euphoria that spoonfuls of Chocolate Explosion Cake can impart? It's a great remedy for anyone in need of a mood adjustment.

The recipes that fill these pages were created to provide you with a primal blast of chocolate to soothe your mind, body, and soul. Chocolate isn't a cure for maladies such as schizophrenia or heart disease, but it sure can have a profound effect on your everyday well-being. So go ahead and indulge—you'll be doing yourself more good than you may know!

Kathy Farrell-Kingsley
rxchoc@aol.com

Before You Start

❖

CHOCOLATE QUESTIONS

HERE'S WHAT YOU NEED TO KNOW TO BUY, store, and use chocolate. And, in case you've ever wondered, I'm also going to tell you how chocolate is made.

What do I need to know when buying chocolate?

Buy chocolate from a reputable merchant with good turnover. Avoid dusty chocolate bars pulled from the back of the shelf: Instead, buy fresh-looking bars that are well wrapped. In some gourmet shops, expensive chocolate is sold in unevenly sized chunks broken from a larger block. This chocolate is usually *couverture chocolate*, which is very high in cocoa butter and is best for candy-making and enrobing, although it can be used for some baking.

In general, bake and cook with what you like to eat. However, do not substitute one kind of chocolate for another in a recipe. If the recipe calls for unsweetened chocolate, bittersweet or semisweet will not work. Milk chocolate, because of its unstable milk solids, is very rarely used for baking and should not be substituted. This is also true for cocoa. If the recipe calls for alkalized, or Dutch processed, cocoa powder, it's worth going to the trouble to find it rather than using natural, or nonalkalized, cocoa powder.

What is the best way to store chocolate?

Store solid chocolate bars and blocks at cool room temperature with moderate humidity (65°F [18°C] and 50 percent humidity are ideal). Wrap them first in aluminum foil and then in plastic. Do not freeze or refrigerate chocolate: The humidity can cause an unsightly sugar bloom and may slightly alter the taste and texture of the chocolate. When correctly stored, dark chocolate will last up to 10 years and milk and white chocolate for 7 to 8 months.

What is tempered chocolate?

When chocolate leaves the factory, it is *tempered*, which means the cocoa-butter crystals are stabilized so that the chocolate shines with its characteristic gloss and breaks with a satisfying snap. Unless the chocolate is improperly stored, it will hold its temper until it is melted for cooking and baking.

How do you chop chocolate?

Use a large sharp knife to chop squares or bars of chocolate. Begin with cool, room-temperature chocolate and chop it on a clean, dry cutting board.

What is the best way to melt chocolate?

Melt chopped chocolate or chocolate chips in the top of a double boiler or in a microwave. Because chocolate burns easily, melt it gently and slowly; the actual temperature of the chocolate during melting should not exceed 100° to 110°F (38° to 43°C). If using a double boiler, set the top portion over water that is barely simmering, because even a droplet of water or a wisp of steam can cause the chocolate to lump and harden, which is known as seizing. The temperature of the water should be between 120° and 140°F (49° to 60°C). To prevent seizing, take care that the water does not touch the bottom of the top portion of the double boiler and that it never boils. When chocolate is melted with cream, butter, or another ingredient, seizing is not a problem, although the water should still be kept at a very low simmer as you melt and stir the chocolate.

To melt chocolate in the microwave, put chopped chocolate pieces or chocolate chips into a microwave-safe container and melt them on medium (50 percent) power, checking after the first minute and then returning the chocolate to the microwave for 20-second intervals, if necessary. Do not expect the chocolate to melt into a liquid pool; instead, it will soften, turn shiny, and become smooth only upon stirring. Keep a close watch, because the chocolate can scorch.

How do I make those fancy chocolate curls used for decorating?

To make decorative chocolate curls, warm a bar or square of chocolate for 20-second intervals in the microwave set on medium (50 percent) power just until it softens but is not melting. Alternatively, hold the chocolate 5 to 6 inches (13 to 15 cm) from a lightbulb for 6 to 7 minutes. Using a paper towel, grip the chocolate at one end and use a vegetable peeler to scrape tight curls onto a baking sheet lined with waxed paper. Refrigerate the curls until you're ready to use them. If the chocolate bar or square is too cool, the peeler will produce shavings rather than curls.

How is chocolate made?

Cacao trees grow in tropical countries on or near the equator. Although native to Central America, the trees thrive in Africa, Indonesia, parts of South America, and even Hawaii. Their cultivation has become a major agricultural endeavor, one that feeds the ever-growing demand for chocolate. The part that is used to make chocolate is the cocoa bean. The beans come from inside pods, which are the fruit of the cacao tree.

Once the cocoa pods are harvested, the beans are scooped out and left in the fields to dry and ferment. Next, they are roasted. Proper roasting is one of the keys to good flavor. After roasting, the beans are shelled and crushed into a meaty mass called nibs. At this point, the nibs are ground into the mass known as chocolate liquor, which is approximately 50 percent cocoa butter. When the chocolate liquor has hardened, it becomes bitter, or unsweetened, chocolate. To make cocoa powder, most of the cocoa butter is extracted and then the liquor is ground and sifted into powder.

During processing, cocoa butter is extracted from chocolate liquor to be used later when manufacturing various sorts of chocolate. For example, semisweet and bittersweet

chocolate are made by blending chocolate liquor with varying amounts of sugar, cocoa butter, flavorings such as
vanilla, and emulsifiers such as lecithin. Milk chocolate is
made much the same way, with the major difference being
that milk solids are added to the chocolate. Premium
chocolate products contain high amounts of cocoa butter
rather than another fat. They also are made from beans that
have been fermented and roasted to a manufacturer's speci-
fications—much like coffee.

Also during processing, chocolate is *conched* and permit-
ted to mellow. Conching is a flavor-developing process that
puts the chocolate through a kneading action between
massive rollers while other ingredients are incorporated.
The longer the chocolate is conched, the finer its final grain
and texture and, in most circumstances, the better the
chocolate is. Chocolate generally is conched for 12 to 72
hours. Following conching, the chocolate goes through a
tempering interval—heating, cooling, and reheating—and
then at last it is ready to be packaged or mixed with other
ingredients to make any number of chocolate and confec-
tionary products.

Though the discovery of chocolate as a drink was made a century earlier by the Spanish court, it wasn't until 1615 that the French became aware of the use of cocoa. That's when Hapsburg-Spanish Princess Anna of Austria married French King Louis XIII and introduced, among other Spanish customs, the drinking of chocolate at the French court. She also gave her betrothed an ornate casket of chocolate.

The Chocolate Emergency Kit

Who can resist chocolate? Melt-in-your-mouth, sweet, velvety chocolate is a sensory experience so satisfying that it drives us to indulgence. Here's the short list of what you should keep on hand, so when the craving strikes, you're at the ready. You can make lots of the recipes in this book with nothing more elaborate than these "chocolate staples":

- Semisweet chocolate chips

- Semisweet chocolate

- Unsweetened chocolate

- Unsweetened cocoa

- Heavy or whipping cream

- Butter

- Flour, all-purpose

- Sugar, granulated

- Baking powder

- Baking soda

15-Minute Tension Tamers

IF YOU'RE FEELING TENSE AND ANXIOUS, TRY THESE *fast stress-busting recipes (each takes 15 minutes or less to prepare)! Chocolate's chemical and sensory properties make it a very appealing, feel-good antidote to stress.*

Mood-enhancing dark chocolate contains tryptophan, an essential amino acid that lessens anxiety by producing the neurotransmitter serotonin. Neurotransmitters are the chemical messengers of the brain. They work by transporting electrical signals between nerve cells. These signals cause changes in the sensations and emotions that we experience, and increased levels of serotonin from eating chocolate bring on feelings of well-being and calm.

Wow! With chocolate readily available, who needs Prozac?

The Recipes

Chocolate Freak-Out

Instant Gratification Chocolate Parfait

Fudgey Caramel Dip

Get Even Truffles

Ooey-Gooey Chocolate Crumble

Easy Street Sandwich Cookies

Edible Dirt

Forever Fondue

Devil's Food Pancakes

Speckled Dutch Baby

Chocolate Clementines

Sisterhood Shake

Wickedly Good Hot Chocolate

Chocolate Martini

Thick Mudslide

Double Chocolate Mochaccino

Stressless Smoothie

Chocolate Freak-Out

When life becomes too much to bear, indulge in this soothing, creamy treat that tastes somewhere between hot chocolate and chocolate pudding. It's really best when served warm. WARNING: The more you eat, the more you'll want.

- 8 ounces (225 g) unsweetened chocolate, finely chopped
- 1 can (14 ounces, or 395 g) sweetened condensed milk
- 2 tablespoons (40 g) light corn syrup
- $1/2$ cup (120 ml) milk, plus more, if needed, to reach desired consistency
- 1 teaspoon (5 ml) vanilla extract
- $1/2$ teaspoon cinnamon

1. In a heavy medium saucepan, combine the chocolate and sweetened condensed milk over low heat, stirring until the chocolate is melted and the mixture is smooth. Stir in the corn syrup until combined.

2. Gradually stir in the milk until well blended. Stir in the vanilla and cinnamon. Stir in additional milk as necessary until the mixture reaches the desired consistency. Serve warm.

YIELD: *About 2 cups (475 ml)*

Even in outer space, chocolate is a favorite treat: Russian and American space flights have always included chocolate.

> *What you see before you, my friend, is the result of a lifetime of chocolate.*

KATHARINE HEPBURN, ACTRESS/WRITER

Instant Gratification Chocolate Parfait

Simple, simple, simple. Tasty, tasty, tasty.

- 4 chocolate graham crackers
- 8 ounces (200 g) whipped cream cheese
- $1/2$ cup (90 g) semisweet chocolate chips, melted and cooled slightly
- 2 tablespoons (25 g) sugar
- $1/2$ cup (125 g) vanilla yogurt
- 2 cups (220 g) fresh raspberries or sliced strawberries

1. Place the crackers into a plastic food-storage bag. Crush them with your fingers or press gently with a rolling pin to make fine crumbs.

2. In a small bowl, mix the cream cheese, cooled chocolate, and sugar. Stir in the yogurt.

3. In tall stemmed glasses, alternate layers of berries, chocolate mixture, crumbs, chocolate mixture, and berries. Serve right away.

YIELD: *4 servings*

Fudgey Caramel Dip

Enjoy your own personal fondue with this fudgey dip. Try it with biscotti, toasted ladyfingers, pound cake cubes, sliced bananas, strawberries, and even nuts. Okay—there's also no harm in just eating it by the spoonful.

- 8 ounces (225 g) semisweet chocolate, chopped
- 4 ounces (115 g) unsweetened chocolate, chopped
- 1^1/$_2$ cups (355 ml) heavy or whipping cream
- 2 tablespoons (^{1}/$_4$ stick, or 30 g) butter
- ^{1}/$_2$ cup (100 g) sugar
- ^{1}/$_8$ teaspoon fresh lemon juice

Milton Hershey became famous for making caramels before he got into the chocolate business. His chocolate proved so popular, however, that he discontinued the caramels.

1. Put the chopped semisweet and unsweetened chocolates in a medium bowl.

2. In a small saucepan, bring the cream and butter to a simmer. Reduce the heat to keep the cream hot but not simmering, until needed.

3. In a medium saucepan, use a whisk to combine the sugar and lemon juice. The sugar will resemble moist sand. Cook the sugar over medium-high heat, stirring constantly with the whisk to break up any lumps, for 7 to 8 minutes. The sugar will become clear as it liquefies, then it will brown as it caramelizes. Remove the saucepan from the heat.

4. Carefully pour about one-third of the hot cream into the caramelized sugar. Whisk the caramel until it stops bubbling, then whisk in the remaining cream until smooth. Immediately pour the hot caramel over the chopped chocolate and let stand for 5 minutes, then whisk until very smooth. Serve immediately.

YIELD: *About 3 cups (705 ml)*

Get Even Truffles

These creamy truffles are custom-made for fans of milk choco-late. Enjoying a few of these may prove to be your best revenge.

- 12 ounces (340 g) milk chocolate, chopped
- 1/3 cup (80 ml) evaporated milk
- 2 cups (200 g) confectioners' sugar
- 1/4 teaspoon salt
- 1 cup (125 g) finely chopped nuts, such as walnuts, almonds, or hazelnuts

1. Melt the chocolate in the top of a double boiler set over simmering (not boiling) water, stirring until smooth. Remove the pan from the water and cool slightly. Or put the chocolate into a microwave-safe bowl and microwave on medium for 2 to 4 minutes, until the chocolate is shiny. Remove from the microwave and stir until smooth and melted. Transfer to a large bowl.

2. Add the evaporated milk, confectioners' sugar, and salt to the chocolate, and beat until well blended.

3. Shape the mixture into 1-inch balls. Roll in the chopped nuts. Chill until ready to eat.

YIELD: *36 truffles*

Ooey-Gooey Chocolate Crumble

A very good friend of mine invented this dish late one night when the urge for something decadent and delicious was strong. Try it, and you'll see that she succeeded, with amazing results.

- 1 cup (235 ml) heavy or whipping cream
- 8 ounces (225 g) semisweet chocolate, finely chopped, or 1$^1/_3$ cups (235 g) semisweet chocolate chips
- 1 teaspoon (5 ml) vanilla extract
- 1 purchased chocolate pound cake (10$^3/_4$ ounces, or 305 g)
- Sweetened whipped cream, for serving

1. In a heavy small saucepan, bring the cream to a simmer. Remove from the heat. Add the chocolate and stir until the mixture is melted and smooth. Stir in the vanilla.

2. To serve, cut the pound cake into cubes. Place the cake cubes into individual serving bowls and spoon the chocolate mixture over the top. Top with whipped cream.

YIELD: *4 servings*

Daniel Peter of Vevey, Switzerland, experimented for eight years before finally inventing a means of making milk chocolate for eating, in 1876.

Easy Street Sandwich Cookies

Your school days may be behind you, but these extremely easy-to-make cookies will take you back. They are a major treat after a hard day in the classroom or office—and don't forget the glass of milk!

- ◆ 4 ounces (100 g) whipped cream cheese
- ◆ 2 tablespoons (25 g) sugar
- ◆ 1/4 cup (45 g) semisweet chocolate chips, melted and cooled slightly
- ◆ 32 chocolate shortbread cookies

1. In a small bowl, mix together the cream cheese, sugar, and melted chocolate.

2. Spread the chocolate mixture on the flat side of half of the cookies. Top with the remaining cookies, flat side down.

YIELD: *16 sandwich cookies*

Chocolate doesn't make the world go round, but it certainly makes the trip worthwhile.

ANONYMOUS

Edible Dirt

You may remember this fun dessert from when you were a child. And even though you're all grown up now, it still tastes good and will satisfy your inner child.

- 4 ounces (115 g) cream cheese, softened
- 2 tablespoons ($1/4$ stick, or 30 g) butter, softened
- 6 tablespoons (40 g) confectioners' sugar
- 1 package (4-serving size) instant chocolate pudding mix
- $1^1/2$ cups (355 ml) cold milk
- 6 ounces (170 g) whipped topping
- 1 package (18 ounces, or 510 grams) Oreo cookies, crushed

1. Using an electric mixer, beat the cream cheese, butter, and confectioners' sugar in a medium bowl until well blended.

2. In a separate medium bowl, whisk together the pudding mix and milk. Fold in the whipped topping.

3. In individual bowls, layer a portion of the crushed cookies, the cream cheese mixture, and the pudding, making several layers of each. End with cookies as the top layer.

YIELD: *4 servings*

Forever Fondue

Sharing a pot of chocolate fondue can really create an intimate mood. Prepare the fondue just before serving, and keep it warm while dipping so that it will remain smooth. Use a traditional fondue pot, or place the pan of fondue on an electric hot plate. Either way, make sure the heat is low; too much heat will cause the chocolate to burn. By the way, fondue lore says if a man loses his morsel while dipping it into the sauce, he has to buy a bottle of wine for the host; a woman who drops her dipper must kiss all of the male guests.

Fondue

- ¹/₂ cup (80 ml) heavy or whipping cream
- 1 teaspoon grated orange zest
- 8 ounces (225 g) bittersweet or semisweet chocolate, finely chopped
- 3 tablespoons (45 ml) Grand Marnier or other orange liqueur

Dippers

- 8 (1-inch or 2.5 cm) pieces pound cake
- 8 (1-inch or 2.5 cm) pieces angel food cake
- 8 fresh strawberries, hulled
- 2 kiwifruit, peeled, each cut into 4 rounds
- 1 small pear, cored, cut into 1-inch (2¹/₂-cm) pieces
- 1 large banana, cut into 8 rounds
- 1 orange, peel and white pith removed, cut into sections
- 8 dried Calimyrna figs
- 8 dried apricot halves

1. In a heavy medium saucepan, bring the cream and orange zest to a simmer. Reduce the heat to low. Add the chocolate and 1 tablespoon (15 ml) of the liqueur and whisk until the mixture is smooth. Remove the fondue from the heat and blend in the remaining 2 tablespoons (30 ml) of liqueur.

2. Transfer the mixture to a fondue pot. Place over a candle or canned heat burner. Alternately, place the saucepan on an electric hot plate. Serve with the dippers.

YIELD: *8 servings*

*Chemically speaking, chocolate
really is the world's perfect food.*

MICHAEL LEVINE, NUTRITION RESEARCHER,
as quoted in *The Emperors of Chocolate: Inside the
Secret World of Hershey and Mars*

Devil's Food Pancakes

These seriously chocolatey pancakes are good eaten any time of the day. Their goodness reaches new heights when topped with the decadent bittersweet sauce. As with all hotcakes, they are best served right off the griddle.

Decadent Sauce

- 7 ounces (200 g) bittersweet chocolate, finely chopped
- 1 cup (235 ml) heavy or whipping cream

Pancakes

- 1¹/4 cups (150 g) all-purpose flour
- 1 cup (200 g) sugar
- ¹/2 cup (45 g) unsweetened cocoa powder
- ¹/2 teaspoon baking soda
- ¹/8 teaspoon salt
- 2 whole large eggs
- 1 large egg yolk
- ³/4 cup (175 ml) buttermilk
- ¹/4 cup (60 ml) vegetable oil
- 1 teaspoon (5 ml) vanilla extract

In a study of 7,800 men, researchers at Harvard University found that men who eat chocolate a few times a month live significantly longer than guys who rarely eat chocolate.

To make the sauce:
1. Put the chocolate into a small bowl. In a small saucepan, bring the cream to a boil, then pour the hot cream over the chocolate, gently whisking until smooth. Keep warm or at room temperature.

To make the pancakes:
1. In a large bowl, sift together the flour, sugar, cocoa, baking soda, and salt. Whisk in the eggs, yolk, buttermilk, oil, and vanilla until well blended.

2. Heat a griddle or nonstick skillet over medium-low heat and lightly coat with butter. Working in batches of two or three, pour $1/4$ cup (about 60 ml) of the batter onto the hot griddle for each pancake and cook until bubbles appear on the surface, 1 to 2 minutes. Flip the pancakes with a large spatula and cook until the tops spring back when pressed gently, about 1 minute more. Transfer to a plate and loosely cover with aluminum foil to keep warm. Continue with the remaining batter, adding $1/2$ teaspoon of butter to the griddle between batches.

3. Serve the pancakes in stacks, topped with the chocolate sauce.

YIELD: *4 servings*

Speckled Dutch Baby

Also called a puffed pancake, this delectable pancake has a lot going for it: It is easy to make and is delicious served for breakfast, brunch, or dessert.

- $1/2$ cup (120 ml) milk
- $1/2$ cup (60 g) all-purpose flour
- $1/4$ cup (50 g) sugar
- 2 large eggs, at room temperature
- 2 tablespoons ($1/4$ stick, or 30 g) butter
- $1/2$ cup (90 g) mini semisweet chocolate chips
- Confectioners' sugar, for dusting

1. Preheat the oven to 425°F (220°C, or gas mark 7). In a medium bowl, whisk together the milk, flour, sugar, and eggs until well blended.

2. In a 10-inch (25-cm) ovenproof skillet, melt the butter over medium heat, tilting the pan to coat the bottom and sides. Pour the batter into the skillet and cook for 1 minute. Do not stir. Sprinkle with the chocolate chips.

3. Transfer the skillet to the oven and bake for 12 to 15 minutes, or until the pancake is puffed and golden. Sprinkle with confectioners' sugar and serve warm.

YIELD: *2 to 4 servings*

Seven billion pounds of chocolate
and chocolate candy are manufactured each
year in the United States.

Chocolate Clementines

This easy treat is not only delicious but refreshing as well. Store the coated clementines in the refrigerator.

- 3¹/₂ ounces (100 g) bittersweet or semisweet chocolate
- 2 ounces (60 ml) orange liqueur, such as Triple Sec or Grand Marnier
- Clementine segments (from about 4 medium clementines)
- ¹/₄ cup (30 g) ground almonds

1. In the top of a double boiler set over simmering (not boiling) water, melt the chocolate with the liqueur. Or place the chocolate and liqueur into a microwave-safe bowl and microwave on medium (50 percent power) for 1¹/₂ to 2 minutes. Stir until the mixture is smooth.

2. Roll the clementine segments in the ground almonds, then dip into the chocolate and place on waxed paper to set.

YIELD: *2 to 4 servings*

Look, there's no metaphysics on earth like chocolates.

FERNANDO PESSOA, PORTUGUESE POET (1888–1935)

Sisterhood Shake

At first glance, this recipe may seem somewhat retro, but it's a fast and furious way to satisfy a chocolate craving. Share it with girlfriends, especially when the letters PMS seem to have a lot of meaning.

- 4 cups (950 ml) cold milk
- 1 package (4-serving size) instant chocolate pudding mix
- $3/4$ teaspoon (5 ml) vanilla extract
- $1/2$ cup ice cubes

1. In a blender, place the milk, pudding mix, and vanilla. Cover and blend until smooth.

2. Add the ice cubes; cover and blend until combined. Let stand 3 minutes to thicken slightly.

3. Pour into tall glasses and serve.

YIELD: *4 to 6 servings*

My tongue is smiling.

ABIGAIL TRILLIN, AGE 4

On finishing a dish of chocolate ice cream, quoted by her father, author Calvin Trillin in Alice Let's Eat.

Wickedly Good Hot Chocolate

The intense chocolate flavor in this recipe comes from using top-quality chocolate rather than cocoa powder.

- $^1/_2$ cup (120 ml) water
- 2 ounces (55 g) bittersweet chocolate, finely chopped
- $3^1/_2$ cups (830 ml) whole milk
- 1 vanilla bean, split lengthwise
- $^1/_3$ cup (65 g) sugar
- $^1/_2$ teaspoon cinnamon
- $^1/_8$ teaspoon salt
- Sweetened whipped cream, for serving

1. In a medium saucepan, bring the water to a boil. Add the chocolate and stir until melted. Remove from the heat.

2. In another medium saucepan, heat the milk with the vanilla bean; cook over moderately high heat until bubbles appear around the edges of the pan. Remove the pan from the heat. Scrape the seeds from the vanilla bean into the hot milk, then discard the bean. Carefully whisk in the sugar, cinnamon, and salt.

3. Pour the hot milk into the melted chocolate and whisk until smooth. Pour the hot chocolate into warm mugs and garnish with a dollop of whipped cream.

YIELD: *4 to 6 servings*

*The divine drink, which builds
up resistance and fights fatigue. A cup
of this precious drink (cocoa) permits a man
to walk for a whole day without food.*

MONTEZUMA, AZTEC EMPEROR (C. 1480–1520)

Chocolate Martini

If you love chocolate and cocktails, you must try this great drink! It puts the "chill" in chilling out. You can use your favorite semisweet, milk, or dark chocolate with great results.

- Ice cubes
- 2 fluid ounces (60 ml) chocolate liqueur
- 1 1/2 fluid ounces (45 ml) vodka
- 1/2 ounce (15 g) grated semisweet, milk, or dark chocolate, for garnish

1. Fill a cocktail shaker with ice. Add the chocolate liqueur and vodka to the shaker. Shake briskly to mix and chill.

2. Strain into two chilled martini glasses. Garnish with the chocolate.

YIELD: *2 servings*

The first chocolate shop opened in London in 1657. Before that, only the nobility could drink chocolate.

Thick Mudslide

Rich and creamy, and oh, soooo good on cold winter days. This is different from the usual hot cocoa—and kids will like it, too.

- 1 cup (85 g) unsweetened cocoa powder
- $^{1}/_{2}$ cup (100 g) sugar
- $^{1}/_{4}$ cup (30 g) all-purpose flour
- $^{1}/_{4}$ cup (30 g) cornstarch
- $4^{1}/_{2}$ cups (1,070 ml) milk

1. In a heavy large saucepan, combine the cocoa, sugar, flour, cornstarch, and milk and cook over medium heat, whisking often, until the mixture comes to a boil. Remove from the heat.

2. Pour the mixture into mugs and serve.

YIELD: *6 to 8 servings*

Aztec emperor Montezuma drank 50 golden goblets of hot chocolate every day. It was thick, dyed red, and flavored with chile peppers. (Now that's hot chocolate!)

Double Chocolate Mochaccino

This sweet hot drink packs a powerful but pleasant punch after a day spent combating the forces of evil. If the forces were particularly evil, add some rum or crème de cacao.

Sweet ground chocolate is available in most supermarkets and gourmet stores.

* 1 cup (235 ml) milk
* 4 tablespoons (20 g) sweet ground chocolate, plus more for garnish
* 1 cup (235 ml) freshly brewed hot espresso

1. In a small bowl or saucepan, whisk together the milk and 2 tablespoons of the ground chocolate until well blended. Make sure there are no lumps.

2. If using a cappuccino machine, steam the milk until it is thick and frothy. Or slowly heat the milk in a small saucepan over low heat, beating with a wire whisk until the milk is hot and foamy.

3. Divide the remaining 2 tablespoons of chocolate between a pair of coffee mugs. Mix half of the espresso into each mug and stir well to make sure the espresso has dissolved any lumps of chocolate.

4. Carefully pour some of the chocolate milk into each espresso-filled cup. With a spoon, gently top each cup with a bit of the foam, taking care not to deflate it by stirring.

5. Garnish each cup with a sprinkling of ground chocolate. Serve right away.

YIELD: *2 servings*

Stressless Smoothie

Quick, easy, and foolproof, this drink will relax your tense muscles in no time.

- 1 cup (235 ml) chocolate milk
- 1/2 cup (75 g) chocolate sorbet
- 2 frozen bananas
- 1 teaspoon (5 ml) vanilla extract

1. In a blender, combine the chocolate milk, sorbet, bananas, and vanilla and process until smooth.

2. Pour into 2 tall glasses and serve.

YIELD: *2 servings*

Chocolate is a perfect food,
as wholesome as it is delicious, a
beneficent restorer of exhausted power. It
is the best friend of those engaged in
literary pursuits.

BARON JUSTUS VON LIEBIG,
GERMAN CHEMIST (1803–1873)

Chocolate causes certain
endocrine glands to secrete hormones
that affect your feelings and behavior
by making you happy. Therefore, it counter-
acts depression, in turn reducing the stress
of depression. Your stress-free life helps
you maintain a youthful disposition,
both physically and mentally. So,
eat lots of chocolate!

ELAINE SHERMAN, AUTHOR
Book of Divine Indulgences

SESSION 2

Chill

STILL FEELING STRESSED? HAVE YOU EVER SEEN PEOPLE
*look stressed when they are eating ice cream? Thought not.
The fact is that a cold sensation in your mouth can release
tension—and it can also help relieve tension headaches. So don't
feel guilty! Put your stress in cold storage with these frozen
chocolate recipes.*

The Recipes

Dark and Delicious Pear Sundaes

When life feels like a never-ending session on the treadmill, this outrageously delicious warm and cold sundae will help you ease the pace. It will not only give you a lift but relieve tension as well.

Chocolate Sauce

*   8 ounces (225 g) bittersweet or semisweet chocolate, coarsely chopped
*   1/3 cup (80 ml) water
*   1/4 cup (50 g) sugar
*   1/4 cup (60 ml) pear liqueur or pear nectar

Pears

*   3 tablespoons (40 g) butter
*   4 small Bosc pears (about 1 pound, or 455 g), peeled, cored, and quartered
*   2 tablespoons (25 g) sugar

*   1 quart (.95 liter) premium chocolate ice cream, softened slightly

To make the sauce:
1. In a small saucepan, combine the chocolate, water, and sugar. Cook over medium-low heat, stirring often, until the chocolate is melted and the mixture is smooth. Remove from the heat and stir in the liqueur. Set aside to cool slightly.

To make the pears:
1. In a large skillet, melt the butter over medium heat. Add the pears and cook, stirring occasionally, for 12 minutes, or until browned and tender, turning once. Add the sugar, stirring gently until the sugar is dissolved and the pears are glazed.

To assemble the sundaes:
1. Place scoops of ice cream in the bottom of individual serving bowls. Spoon 2 pear pieces and some of their sauce around the ice cream in each bowl. Top with chocolate sauce.

YIELD: *6 to 8 servings*

A 1½-ounce (45 g) square of dark chocolate may have as many cancer-fighting antioxidants as a 5-ounce (150 ml) glass of red wine.

Chocolate Waffle Sundaes

Say goodbye to stress and anxiety in one of the most delicious ways I know, by treating yourself with this irresistible chocolate-studded sundae.

Chocolate Waffles

- 1 cup (200 g) sugar
- 1^1/4 cups (150 g) unbleached all-purpose flour
- ^{1}/3 cup (30 g) unsweetened cocoa powder
- 1^1/2 teaspoons baking powder
- ^{1}/2 teaspoon baking soda
- ^{1}/4 teaspoon salt
- 2^1/2 ounces (70 g) unsweetened chocolate, chopped
- 3 tablespoons (40 g) butter
- 2 tablespoons (28 ml) vegetable oil
- 1^1/2 teaspoons (7 ml) vanilla extract
- 2 teaspoons instant coffee granules or powder dissolved in 6 tablespoons (90 ml) warm water
- 2 large eggs
- 1^1/3 cups (315 g) buttermilk

Assembly Ingredients

- Confectioners' sugar
- Chocolate ice cream
- 1 recipe Decadent Fudge Sauce (page 92)
- English toffee bits
- Chopped nuts, toasted

To make the waffles:

1. In a large bowl, combine the sugar, flour, cocoa, baking powder, baking soda, and salt. Set aside.

2. In a heavy medium saucepan over medium-low heat, combine the chocolate and butter and stir until melted and smooth. Remove the pan from the heat and whisk in the oil, vanilla, and coffee mixture. Let cool to lukewarm. Whisk in the eggs and buttermilk until well blended.

3. Stir the chocolate mixture into the dry ingredients until well blended.

4. Preheat a waffle iron to medium heat following the manufacturer's instructions. Pour about $1/2$ to $3/4$ cup (115 to 170 g) of batter (depending on the size of the waffle iron) into the center of the waffle iron; spread evenly with a spatula. Close the waffle iron and cook until the waffle is cooked through but still soft and the surface has darkened, about 4 minutes (time will vary, depending on the waffle iron). Using a spatula, transfer the waffle to a rack. Repeat with the remaining batter to make 9 waffles total.

To assemble the sundaes:

1. Cut each waffle diagonally in half, forming triangles. Arrange 3 waffle triangles on each of 6 plates. Dust with confectioners' sugar. Place a scoop of ice cream over the waffle triangles. Pour the sauce over the waffles and ice cream. Sprinkle with toffee bits and chopped nuts.

YIELD: *6 servings*

Decadent Fudge Sauce

This thick, glossy sauce makes chocolate syrup taste ho-hum. It's wonderful poured over any flavor of ice cream to create a luscious hot fudge sundae. This sauce will harden and turn chewy as it comes in contact with cold ice cream, just like the old-fashioned hot fudge.

- 2 ounces (55 g) unsweetened chocolate, coarsely chopped
- 2 tablespoons (1/4 stick, or 30 g) butter
- 1/2 cup (120 ml) boiling water
- 1 cup (200 g) sugar
- 1 tablespoon (5 g) unsweetened cocoa powder
- 2 tablespoons (40 g) light corn syrup
- 2 teaspoons (10 ml) vanilla extract

Cole Porter got a kick from fudge.
He had 9 pounds of it shipped to him each
month from his hometown.

1. In a heavy medium saucepan, combine the chocolate and butter. Cook over medium-low heat, stirring often, until the mixture is melted and smooth.

2. Slowly stir in the boiling water, then the sugar, cocoa, and corn syrup. Bring the mixture to a boil over medium heat, stirring often. Reduce the heat to medium-low and simmer, without stirring, for 8 to 9 minutes.

3. Remove from the heat and let cool for 5 minutes. Stir in the vanilla.

4. Serve right away, or pour into an airtight container and refrigerate for up to 2 weeks. Reheat in a saucepan over low heat, or microwave in a microwave-safe bowl, loosely covered, on medium-low power for 1 to 2 minutes, stirring once.

YIELD: *1 1/2 cups (295 ml)*

A plain milk chocolate candy bar has more protein than a banana.

Chocolate Decadence Ice Cream Pie

Sometimes when the going gets rough, even the most grown-up, well-adjusted, and emotionally mature people can start feeling like they want to throw a tantrum. That's when it's time to indulge your inner child with a decadent ice cream pie made with three kinds of ice cream (all chocolate), chocolate sauce, and a chocolate cookie crust. One bite will put you back on the fast track to happiness.

Crust

- 1¹/₂ cups (170 g) finely ground or crushed chocolate wafer cookies
- 6 tablespoons (³/₄ stick, or 85 g) butter, melted

Chocolate Sauce

- ³/₄ cup (175 ml) heavy or whipping cream
- 2 tablespoons (¹/₄ stick, or 30 g) unsalted butter
- 2 tablespoons (40 g) light corn syrup
- 8 ounces (225 g) bittersweet or semisweet chocolate, chopped
- 1 teaspoon (5 ml) vanilla extract

Filling

- 2 pints (570 g) chocolate-chocolate chip ice cream
- 1 pint (285 g) chocolate fudge brownie ice cream
- 1 pint (285 g) cookies-and-cream ice cream
- 2 ounces (55 g) white chocolate, melted

To make the crust:

1. Preheat the oven to 325°F (170°C, or gas mark 3). Coat a 9-inch (22½-cm) pie pan with cooking spray.

2. In a medium bowl, mix the cookie crumbs and melted butter to form fine crumbs. Press the mixture firmly onto the bottom and up the sides of the prepared pan. Bake until the crust is set, about 10 minutes. Let cool completely.

To make the chocolate sauce:

1. In a medium saucepan, combine the cream, butter, and corn syrup and bring to a simmer. Remove from the heat.

2. Add the chocolate and let stand for 1 minute. Whisk the mixture until melted and smooth. Stir in the vanilla. Let stand at room temperature until cool and slightly thickened, about 20 minutes.

To assemble the pie:

1. Place alternate scoops of chocolate-chocolate chip ice cream, chocolate fudge brownie ice cream, and cookies-and-cream ice cream in a single layer in the cooled crust and flatten slightly. Drizzle ½ cup of chocolate sauce over the ice cream. Freeze the pie until the sauce sets, about 10 minutes. Top the pie with scoops of the remaining ice cream, alternating the flavors and mounding in the center. Drizzle ⅓ cup of the chocolate sauce over the top. Freeze the pie until firm, at least 2 hours.

2. Using a small spoon, drizzle the melted white chocolate in thin lines over the ice cream pie. Freeze until the white chocolate is firm, about 10 minutes.

3. Stir the remaining chocolate sauce over low heat just until warm. Serve the pie with the warm chocolate sauce.

YIELD: *10 servings*

Chocolate Macaroon Ice Cream Cake

Just about everyone likes a cake made with ice cream, and this dessert will be no exception. One great thing about ice cream cakes is that they can be made with any flavor of ice cream, which allows you to create a personalized version.

- 1 package (13 ounces, or 370 g) soft coconut macaroons
- 2 pints (570 g) chocolate ice cream, slightly softened
- 2 pints (570 g) coffee or vanilla ice cream, slightly softened
- 1/2 cup (120 ml) purchased chocolate shell ice cream topping
- 1 cup (125 g) chopped walnuts, toasted

Life is like a box of chocolates . . . full of nuts!

BUMPER STICKER

1. Lightly coat an 8 x 3-inch (20 x 7^1/2-cm) springform pan with cooking spray. Break up half of the macaroons to make coarse crumbs. Lightly press the crumbs over the bottom and ^{1}/2 inch (1^1/2 cm) up the sides of the pan. Spread the chocolate ice cream evenly over the crust.

2. Break the remaining macaroons into coarse crumbs. Sprinkle them evenly over the chocolate ice cream. Freeze for about 45 minutes, or until almost firm.

3. Spread the coffee or vanilla ice cream evenly over top of the cake and freeze for at least 4 hours, or until firm.

4. Pour the chocolate topping on the middle of the cake and tilt the pan to cover the top completely. Let the topping harden for about 5 minutes.

5. Wrap the pan with a warm, damp kitchen towel for 1 minute to loosen the sides. Remove the springform from the cake's sides and pat the nuts onto the sides of the cake. (If the ice cream is too hard for the walnuts to stick, leave the cake at room temperature for 5 to 10 minutes, then apply them.)

YIELD: *10 to 12 servings*

Never mind about 1066
William the Conqueror, 1087 William
the Second. Such things are not going to
affect one's life...but 1932 the Mars Bar
and 1936 Maltesers and 1937 the Kit
Kat——these dates are milestones in history
and should be seared into the memory of
every child in the country.

ROALD DAHL, AUTHOR,
Charlie and the Chocolate Factory

Fudgewiches

Chocolate ice cream, chocolate cookies, and a fudgey topping all combine for decadent ice cream sandwiches that will be a hit with kids and adults alike.

- 2 tablespoons (25 g) sugar
- 2 tablespoons (40 g) light corn syrup
- 1 1/2 tablespoons (10 g) unsweetened cocoa powder
- 1 tablespoon (15 ml) milk
- 1 teaspoon (5 g) butter
- 1 teaspoon (5 ml) vanilla extract
- 1 1/4 cups (175 g) chocolate ice cream (or your favorite flavor), softened slightly
- 20 chocolate wafer cookies

1. In a heavy small saucepan, combine the sugar, corn syrup, cocoa, and milk. Bring to a boil over medium-low heat, whisking constantly. Cook for 2 minutes or until thick, whisking frequently. Remove from the heat and stir in the butter and vanilla. Cover and chill thoroughly.

2. Spread 2 tablespoons of the ice cream onto each of 10 cookies; top each with about 1 teaspoon of the chocolate syrup and a remaining cookie, pressing gently. Freeze for at least 1 hour. Serve frozen.

YIELD: *10 sandwiches*

Black-and-White
Ice Cream Sandwiches

If you serve these ice cream sandwiches after dinner, by midnight you may discover that several members of your family have tiptoed into the kitchen for "just one more." Chocolate ice cream is the filling between tender chocolate cookies that have been dipped halfway into white chocolate. Let's face it: Those who eat chocolate on a regular basis are those who enjoy life.

- 2 pints (570 g) chocolate ice cream, softened slightly
- 1^1/4 cups (150 g) all-purpose flour
- ^{1}/4 cup (20 g) unsweetened cocoa powder
- ^{1}/4 teaspoon salt
- ^{3}/4 cup (1^1/2 sticks, 165 g) butter, softened
- ^{1}/2 cup plus 2 tablespoons (125 g) sugar
- 1 large egg yolk
- 1 teaspoon (5 ml) vanilla extract
- 10 ounces (280 g) white chocolate, chopped

1. Drop six ^{2}/3-cup (95-g) mounds of chocolate ice cream on a baking sheet lined with waxed paper. Using a metal spatula, shape each mound into a 3- to 3^1/2-inch (7^1/2- to 9-cm) square and freeze.

2. Sift together the flour, cocoa, and salt; set aside.

3. In a large bowl, using an electric mixer, beat the butter and sugar until smooth. Beat in the egg yolk and vanilla. Beat in the flour mixture until blended and a soft dough forms. Gather the dough into a ball and flatten into a rectangle.

4. Place the dough between 2 sheets of waxed paper and roll it out into a 13 x 10-inch (32^1/$_2$ x 25-cm) rectangle. Place the dough, still between waxed paper sheets, on a baking sheet. Chill until firm, at least 1 hour and up to 1 day.

5. Preheat the oven to 300°F (150°C, or gas mark 2). Line a large baking sheet with parchment paper. Peel the top sheet of the waxed paper off the dough. Trim the dough to a 12 x 9-inch (30 x 22^1/$_2$-inch) rectangle; cut the dough into twelve 3-inch (7^1/$_2$-cm) squares. Transfer the squares to the parchment-lined baking sheet, spacing them about 1 inch (2^1/$_2$ cm) apart. Bake until the cookies are firm to the touch, about 20 minutes. Cool the cookies completely on the sheet.

6. Melt the white chocolate in the top of a double boiler set over barely simmering (not boiling) water, stirring until smooth. Remove the pan from over the water.

7. Holding the corner of 1 cookie, dip the cookie into the melted chocolate until it's half-covered on a diagonal, tilting the pan if necessary to submerge. Shake the cookie gently to allow some of the excess chocolate to drip back into the pan. Return the dipped cookie to the baking sheet. Repeat with the remaining cookies and white chocolate. Freeze the cookies until the chocolate coating is firm, about 10 minutes.

8. Arrange 6 cookies, flat side up, on a work surface. Top each with a frozen ice cream square, then another cookie, flat side down, pressing slightly to adhere. Cover and freeze the sandwiches. Serve frozen.

YIELD: *6 sandwiches*

Velvety Chocolate Ice Cream

On a warm, sunny day—or actually, any day—there's no dessert more satisfying than ice cream. Of course, it can't be just any ice cream. It must be one that's remarkably rich, ultra-creamy, and made with premium chocolate. And while you can happily consume ice cream this good plain, I have made an important discovery: You can reach new heights of nirvana when you top this with Decadent Fudge Sauce (pages 54-55).

- 3 large egg yolks
- 1³/4 cups (425 ml) milk
- ¹/2 cup (100 g) sugar
- ²/3 cup (4 ounces, or 115 g) semisweet chocolate chips
- 1 ounce (30 g) unsweetened chocolate, coarsely chopped
- 1 cup (235 ml) heavy or whipping cream
- 1 teaspoon (5 ml) vanilla extract

1. In a small bowl, whisk the egg yolks until blended.

2. In a medium saucepan, stir the milk and sugar over medium heat until the mixture comes to a gentle boil. Whisk about $1/2$ cup into the yolks, then whisk the yolk mixture into the saucepan. Whisk constantly over medium-low heat until the mixture looks as if it's just about to boil, 1 to 2 minutes.

3. Remove the saucepan from the heat and add the semisweet and unsweetened chocolates, stirring until melted.

4. Stir in the cream and vanilla. Refrigerate for 20 minutes.

5. Pour into an ice cream maker and freeze according to the manufacturer's instructions. Serve right away or pack into an airtight freezer container and freeze for up to 1 month.

YIELD: *4 cups (560 g)*

*Other things are just food.
But chocolate's chocolate.*

PATRICK SKENE CATLING, AUTHOR,
The Chocolate Touch

Change-Your-World Tartufo

This is the stuff that dreams are made of: two flavors of ice cream, whipped cream, melted chocolate, cherries, and almonds. The flavors are pure and simple. It's just the thing to surprise a special friend who needs some cheering up.

- 2 pints (570 g) cherry vanilla ice cream, softened slightly
- 1 cup (125 g) chopped almonds, toasted
- 1^1/2 pints (430 g) chocolate-chocolate chip ice cream, softened slightly
- 1^1/2 cups (355 ml) whipping cream
- ^{1}/4 cup (80 g) light corn syrup
- 24 ounces (680 g) bittersweet (not unsweetened) or semisweet chocolate, chopped
- 6 ounces (170 g) semisweet chocolate, chopped
- 2 teaspoons (10 ml) vanilla extract

1. Line a 9 x 5 x 2^1/2-inch (22^1/2 x 13 x 6^1/2-cm) metal loaf pan with plastic wrap, leaving a 3-inch (7^1/2-cm) overhang on all sides. Using a small, flexible spatula, quickly spread the softened cherry vanilla ice cream evenly over the bottom and up the sides of the prepared pan. Freeze until firm, about 30 minutes.

2. Sprinkle ^{1}/4 cup (30 g) of the chopped almonds over the ice cream in the bottom of the pan. Spread the softened chocolate-chocolate chip ice cream over the almonds, filling the pan completely. Freeze until the ice cream is firm, about 1 hour.

3. In a medium saucepan, bring the cream and the corn syrup to a simmer. Remove from the heat. Add the bittersweet and semisweet chocolates and whisk until smooth. Whisk in the vanilla. Cool to room temperature, about 45 minutes, whisking occasionally.

4. Spread $2/3$ cup (160 ml) of the chocolate mixture over the top of the ice cream. Freeze until the chocolate is very firm, about 2 hours.

5. Rewarm the remaining chocolate mixture over low heat just until fluid (if necessary). Line a baking sheet with waxed paper. Run a small knife around the sides of the loaf pan to loosen the ice cream loaf. Invert the loaf onto the prepared sheet; peel off the plastic wrap.

6. Working quickly and using a small, flexible spatula, spread 1 cup (235 ml) of the chocolate mixture over the top and sides of the ice cream loaf, covering the ice cream completely and forming a $1/4$-inch-thick ($1/2$-cm) coating (reserve the remaining chocolate). Sprinkle the remaining $3/4$ cup (95 g) of chopped almonds over the top and sides of the chocolate-covered ice cream loaf. Freeze until the chocolate is firm, about 1 hour.

7. To serve, cut the tartufo into $1/2$-inch-thick ($1 1/2$-cm) slices. Cut each slice diagonally in half, forming 2 triangles. Place 2 triangles on each plate. If desired, serve with the remaining rewarmed chocolate mixture.

YIELD: *8 to 10 servings*

Frozen Chocolate Bombe

Here's an impressive dessert—and a breeze to put together. The bombe is just a layering of purchased ice cream, sorbet, and cookies, and it's topped off with a store-bought fudge sauce spruced up with chocolate chips.

- 1 jar (16 ounces, or 455 g) purchased hot fudge sauce
- 2 cups (350 g) semisweet chocolate chips
- 3 tablespoons (45 ml) water
- 2 teaspoons (10 ml) vanilla extract
- 3 pints (855 g) vanilla ice cream with chocolate chunks, softened slightly
- 1$^1/_2$ pints (430 g) chocolate sorbet, softened slightly
- 1 package (9 ounces, or 255 g) chocolate wafer cookies

1. In a heavy medium saucepan, combine the fudge sauce, chocolate chips, and water. Cook over medium-low heat, stirring often, until the mixture is melted and smooth. Remove from the heat. Whisk in the vanilla and let cool.

2. Line a 10-inch-diameter (25-cm), 10-cup (2,375-ml) metal bowl with plastic wrap, extending it over the sides. Spread the vanilla ice cream over the inside of the bowl to within $^3/_4$ inch (2 cm) of the top edge, leaving a 6-inch (15-cm) hollow cavity in the center. Freeze for 30 minutes.

3. Fill the center completely with the sorbet and smooth the top. Overlap half of the cookies (about 22) over the ice cream and sorbet, covering it completely and pressing gently. Spread 1¹/₂ cups (350 ml) of the chocolate mixture over the cookies. Overlap the remaining cookies over the sauce. Cover and freeze overnight. Cover and chill the remaining sauce.

4. To serve, rewarm the remaining sauce over low heat, stirring often. Turn the bombe out onto a platter. Peel off the plastic. Cut the bombe into wedges. Serve with the warm sauce.

YIELD: *10 to 12 servings*

Chocolate is a fabulous energy source. Just one chocolate chip provides enough food energy for an adult to walk 150 feet.

Bittersweet Granita

Dark, delicious, and more decadent than icy, this chocolate delicacy has a sorbetlike quality.

- 4 cups (950 ml) water
- 2/3 cup (135 g) sugar
- 1 cup (85 g) unsweetened cocoa powder
- Fresh mint sprigs, for garnish
- Sweetened whipped cream (optional)

1. In a medium saucepan, combine the water, sugar, and cocoa. Cook over medium-low heat just until the mixture starts to bubble at the edges. Cook, whisking, until slightly thickened, about 1 minute. Remove from the heat and let cool.

2. Pour the granita mixture into a wide and shallow container, such as a stainless-steel baking dish (the shallower the container, the quicker the granita will freeze). Cover with a lid, aluminum foil, or plastic wrap. Freeze the mixture for 1 to 2 hours, until it is solid around the edges. Take the container out of the freezer and scrape the granita with a fork, mixing it from the edges into the center.

3. Repeat this scraping and mixing process every 30 minutes or so (at least 3 times) until the entire mixture has turned into small, sequined ice flakes.

4. When ready to serve, "rake" with a fork to loosen the granita, and spoon into serving dishes. Garnish with mint sprigs and serve with whipped cream, if desired.

YIELD: *1 quart*

Shameless Chocolate Shake

The next time you find yourself on the edge, think fast and whip up this thick and intoxicating drink. It's sure to melt away anxiety and leave you with a lasting happy impression.

- $1/2$ cup (115 g) sour cream or crème fraîche
- $1/4$ cup (60 ml) dark, bittersweet, or triple chocolate-flavored syrup
- $1^1/2$ pints (430 g) chocolate ice cream, softened
- Ground cinnamon (optional)

1. In a blender, combine the sour cream and the chocolate syrup. Cover and blend until smooth, stopping the blender and scraping down the sides if necessary. Add the ice cream and blend until smooth, scraping down the sides of the blender.

2. Pour the shake into glasses. If desired, sprinkle the top of each with cinnamon. Serve right away.

YIELD: *2 to 4 servings*

There are four basic food groups: milk chocolate, dark chocolate, white chocolate, and chocolate truffles.

ANONYMOUS

Chocolate Ice Cubes

The ways you can use these ice cubes are endless: in iced coffee, iced tea, seltzer, shakes, soda, and so on, whenever you need a chocolate lift.

- $^1/_2$ cup (100 g) sugar
- $^3/_4$ cup (175 ml) water
- $^1/_2$ cup (45 g) unsweetened cocoa powder
- $^1/_4$ cup (45 g) mini semisweet chocolate chips

1. In a medium saucepan, combine the sugar and water and bring to a boil over medium-high heat. Remove the pan from the heat and whisk in the cocoa until smooth. Add the chocolate chips and stir until completely melted.

2. Lightly coat an ice cube tray with cooking spray. Pour the mixture into the prepared ice cube tray and freeze until firm.

YIELD: *About 12 ice cubes*

*Exercise is a dirty word.
Every time I hear it, I wash my
mouth out with chocolate.*

CHARLES M. SCHULZ, CARTOONIST
Creator of *Peanuts* comic strip

Chocolate Comfort Foods

WHEN YOU DON'T NEED A FAST FIX AND YOU'RE NOT IN *the mood for cold comfort, no therapy is effective as good old comfort food. There's something so warm and relaxing about chocolate childhood favorites. Perhaps it's because the tastes and smells bring you back to a world of certainties and simplicity, comfort and security. Everyone has his or her own favorite, of course. But whether yours is luscious bread pudding or rich, fudgey brownies, take yourself back to a stress-free time with these decadent treats. When you return to the real world, you'll be ready to handle anything.*

The Recipes

Killer Brownies

Chocolate Chubbies

Make-a-Comeback Chocolatey Cookies

Shortbread Fudge Layer

Heavenly Bittersweet Rice Pudding

Chocolate Bread Pudding

Outrageous Warm Chocolate Pudding

Chocolate Pie Pastry

Charleston Chocolate Pecan Pie

Mud Pie

Sky-High Chocolate Pie

You-Deserve-It Chocolate Cake with Glossy Glaze

Chocolate Pudding Cake

Nostalgic Chocolate Cupcakes

Molten Chocolate Cakes

The Devil's Angel Food Cake

Blackout Cake

Intense Chocolate Loaf

Triple Chocolate Cheesecake

Killer Brownies

These decadent, super-chocolatey brownies are top-quality lick-the-bowl material and a surefire cure for a serious chocolate craving.

- 1¼ cups (150 g) all-purpose flour
- ¼ teaspoon salt
- ¼ teaspoon baking soda
- ½ cup (1 stick, or 110 g) butter, softened
- 2 ounces (55 g) unsweetened chocolate, chopped
- 3 ounces (85 g) bittersweet chocolate, chopped
- 2 large eggs
- 1 cup (225 g) packed light brown sugar
- 2 tablespoons (40 g) corn syrup
- 1 teaspoon (5 ml) vanilla extract
- 1 cup (175 g) mini semisweet chocolate chips

The first mention of brownies in print was in 1897, when they were listed for sale in the Sears, Roebuck, and Company catalog.

1. Preheat the oven to 350°F (180°C, or gas mark 4). Coat an 8-inch (20-cm) square baking pan with cooking spray.

2. In a small bowl, mix the flour, salt, and baking soda.

3. In a medium saucepan, combine the butter and unsweetened and bittersweet chocolates. Place over low heat and stir occasionally until melted. Let cool 10 minutes.

4. Meanwhile, in a medium bowl, using an electric mixer on medium, beat the eggs, brown sugar, and corn syrup until well blended. Beat in the vanilla, then add the chocolate mixture and beat just until blended. With a wooden spoon, stir in the flour mixture. Stir in $3/4$ cup (130 g) of the chocolate chips.

5. Spread the batter evenly into the prepared pan. Sprinkle the top with the remaining chips. Bake for 30 to 35 minutes, or until a toothpick inserted into the center comes out moist, not wet. Set the pan on a wire rack. Cool the brownies completely in the pan before cutting into bars.

YIELD: *20 bars*

Chocolate Chubbies

Chock-full of chocolate chunks, these cookies deliver mouthfuls of melting chocolate in every bite. You can buy bags of chocolate chunks near the chocolate chips in your market, or you can coarsely chop a bar of semisweet chocolate.

- $2/3$ cup (10 tablespoons plus 2 teaspoons, or 150 g) butter, softened
- $2/3$ cup (135 g) granulated sugar
- $1/3$ cup (75 g) packed light brown sugar
- 1 large egg
- 1 teaspoon (5 ml) vanilla extract
- $1^1/2$ cups (180 g) all-purpose flour
- $1^1/2$ cups (275 g) semisweet chocolate chunks
- 1 cup (125 g) chopped walnuts (optional)

1. Preheat the oven to 325°F (170°C, or gas mark 3). Lightly coat 2 baking sheets with cooking spray.

2. In a large bowl, using an electric mixer, beat the butter, granulated sugar, brown sugar, egg, and vanilla until pale and fluffy. With the mixer on low speed, gradually add the flour, beating just until blended. Stir in the chocolate chunks and walnuts, if using.

3. Drop heaping tablespoonfuls of dough $2^1/2$ inches ($6^1/2$ cm) apart onto the prepared baking sheets.

4. Bake for 17 minutes, or until the tops look dry. Cool the cookies on the baking sheets on wire racks for 5 minutes before removing the cookies to the racks to cool completely.

YIELD: *36 cookies*

Don't wreck a sublime chocolate experience by feeling guilty. Chocolate isn't like premarital sex. It will not make you pregnant. And it always feels good.

LORA BRODY,
CELEBRITY CHEF/COOKBOOK AUTHOR

Make-a-Comeback Chocolatey Cookies

Make a batch of this cookie dough, and keep it in the freezer or refrigerator so it's close at hand when you need something deep and decadent to ward off an existential crisis.

- 1 cup (2 sticks, or 225 g) butter, softened
- 1¹/₄ cups (250 g) sugar
- ¹/₂ teaspoon baking soda
- 1 large egg
- 2 cups (240 g) all-purpose flour
- ¹/₂ cup (45 g) unsweetened cocoa powder
- ¹/₂ cup (90 g) mini semisweet chocolate chips
- ¹/₂ cup (75 g) finely chopped walnuts (optional)

The Swiss lead the world in annual per capita chocolate consumption: They consume chocolate at the rate of approximately 22 pounds (about 10 kilograms) per person per year.

1. In a large bowl, using an electric mixer on medium, beat the butter, sugar, and baking soda until fluffy. Beat in the egg. With the mixer on low speed, beat in the flour and cocoa, half at a time, until blended. Stir in the chocolate chips.

2. Divide the dough in half. Roll each half on a lightly floured surface into a 7-inch (17^1/2-cm) log. Roll each log in the nuts, if using, until the logs are 10 inches (25 cm) long. Wrap each in plastic wrap. Refrigerate for at least 4 hours until firm, or up to 1 week.

3. Preheat the oven to 350°F (180°C, or gas mark 4). Coat 2 baking sheets with cooking spray. Cut the logs into ^{1}/2-inch (1^1/2-cm) slices. Place the slices 1 inch (2^1/2 cm) apart on the baking sheets.

4. Bake for 8 to 10 minutes, just until the cookies are set and the tops look dry. Let cool a few minutes on the baking sheets before removing to wire racks to cool completely.

YIELD: *40 cookies*

Shortbread Fudge Layer Bars

These delectable bars begin with a layer of shortbread pastry that is baked twice—once alone, and again with a topping of brownie batter.

Crust

- $1/2$ cup (1 stick, or 110 g) butter, softened
- 1 cup (120 g) all-purpose flour
- $1/4$ cup (50 g) sugar
- $1/4$ teaspoon salt

Topping

- $1/2$ cup (1 stick, or 110 g) butter, softened
- 3 ounces (85 g) unsweetened chocolate, chopped
- 2 large eggs
- $3/4$ cup (150 g) sugar
- 3 tablespoons (25 g) all-purpose flour
- $1/2$ teaspoon baking powder

It's rumored that Napoleon carried chocolate with him on all of his military campaigns for a quick energy boost.

To make the crust:

1. Preheat the oven to 350°F (180°C, or gas mark 4). Coat an 11 x 7-inch (28 x 17^1/2-cm) baking pan with cooking spray.

2. In a food processor or with an electric mixer, process or beat the butter, flour, sugar, and salt until the mixture holds together and forms a dough. Press into the bottom of the pre-pared pan. Bake for 20 minutes or until light golden and firm when touched. Remove from the oven but do not turn the oven off.

To make the topping:

1. In a small saucepan, heat the butter and chocolate over low heat, stirring often, until melted. Let cool for 5 minutes.

2. In a medium bowl, whisk together the eggs, sugar, flour, and baking powder until blended. Whisk in the cooled choco-late mixture. Pour the batter over the crust in the pan.

3. Bake for 20 minutes, or until the top feels firm. Let cool in the pan before cutting into bars.

YIELD: *24 bars*

Around 1,000 A.D., all taxes were
paid in cocoa beans to feudal Aztecs.

Heavenly Bittersweet Rice Pudding

Reach for this recipe to chase away the blues, bring sunshine to a dreary day, or let family and friends know you're glad they're around.

- 4 large eggs, slightly beaten
- 2 cups (475 ml) half-and-half, light cream, or whole milk
- 1/3 cup (75 g) sugar
- 1/4 cup (20 g) unsweetened cocoa powder
- 1 teaspoon (5 ml) vanilla extract
- 1 cup (175 g) cooked rice, cooled
- 2 ounces (55 g) semisweet chocolate, chopped
- 2 ounces (55 g) bittersweet chocolate, chopped

1. Preheat the oven to 325°F (170°C, or gas mark 3). In a large bowl, whisk together the eggs, half-and-half, sugar, cocoa, and vanilla. Stir in the rice and both chocolates. Pour the custard mixture into a 1¹/2- or 2-quart (1¹/2- or 2-liter) casserole. Place the dish in a 13 x 9 x 2-inch (32¹/2 x 22¹/2 x 5-cm) baking pan set on an oven rack. Carefully pour 1 inch (2¹/2 cm) of boiling water into the baking pan.

2. Bake, uncovered, for 60 to 65 minutes, or until a knife inserted near the center comes out clean.

3. To serve, spoon the warm pudding into bowls.

YIELD: *6 to 8 servings*

Chocolate Bread Pudding

Food philosophers like to say that bread sustains life and chocolate makes it worth living. Here's a pudding that combines the two, with delicious results. Store the bread pudding tightly covered in the refrigerator for up to 5 days. Bring to room temperature or warm in the oven before serving.

- $^3/_4$ cup (150 g) sugar
- $^1/_3$ cup (30 g) unsweetened cocoa powder
- $^1/_2$ teaspoon instant coffee granules or powder
- 2 cups (475 ml) milk
- 2 tablespoons ($^1/_4$ stick, or 30 g) butter
- 3 large eggs
- 4 slices firm white bread, cut into $^1/_2$-inch ($1^1/_2$-cm) cubes
- $^3/_4$ cup (130 g) mini semisweet chocolate chips

There are two kinds of people in the world.
Those who love chocolate, and communists.

LESLIE MOAK MURRAY, CARTOONIST

in *Murray's Law* comic strip

1. Preheat the oven to 350°F (180°C, or gas mark 4). In a medium saucepan, whisk together the sugar, cocoa, and coffee until blended. Whisk in 1 cup of the milk. Cook over medium heat, whisking often, for 2 to 3 minutes, until the mixture comes to a boil and the sugar dissolves.

2. Remove the saucepan from the heat and whisk in the butter until melted. Whisk in the remaining 1 cup of milk, then the eggs, until blended. Stir in the bread and chocolate chips. Pour into a $1^1/2$- to 2-quart ($1^1/2$- to 2-liter) baking dish.

3. Place the dish in a 13 x 9 x 2-inch ($32^1/2$ x $22^1/2$ x 5-cm) baking pan. Add 1 inch ($2^1/2$ cm) of hot water to the pan.

4. Bake until a knife inserted near the center comes out clean, 50 to 60 minutes. Remove the dish from the water and place it on a wire rack until it reaches the desired serving temperature. Serve warm, at room temperature, or chilled.

YIELD: *6 servings*

Outrageous Warm Chocolate Pudding

This comforting dessert will appeal to all ages. The flavor is rich, the texture is smooth, and no one will be able to pass it up! Top with whipped cream, if desired.

- 4 teaspoons plus $^1/_3$ cup (80 g) sugar
- 8 ounces (225 g) bittersweet chocolate, chopped
- $^1/_4$ cup ($^1/_2$ stick, or 55 g) butter
- 4 large egg yolks
- 2 teaspoons (10 ml) vanilla extract
- 7 large egg whites
- $^1/_2$ teaspoon salt

Chocolate was first introduced in the United States in 1765, by Irish chocolate-maker John Hanan. Hanan teamed up with Dr. James Baker, and together, they built America's first chocolate factory. By 1780, the pair was making the famous Baker's chocolate, which is still sold today.

1. Preheat the oven to 350°F (180°C, or gas mark 4). Coat 4 individual 6- to 8-ounce (175- to 235-ml) custard cups or ramekins with cooking spray and dust each with 1 teaspoon (4 g) of the sugar. Set them in a baking pan large enough to hold them snugly.

2. Melt the chocolate in the top of a double boiler set over simmering (not boiling) water, stirring until smooth. Remove the pan from the water and beat in the remaining $^1/_3$ cup (65 g) of sugar and the butter until blended. Beat in the egg yolks one at a time and then beat in the vanilla.

3. In a medium bowl using an electric mixer, beat the egg whites and salt until stiff peaks form. Fold the egg whites into the chocolate mixture, then spoon the mixture into the pre-pared cups.

4. Add enough hot water to the baking pan to come halfway up the sides of the cups. Bake for 25 minutes, or until the tops are firm to the touch. Remove to a wire rack and let cool slightly. Serve warm.

YIELD: *4 servings*

Chocolate Pie Pastry

This all-purpose piecrust recipe can be used in place of a regular crust in just about any dessert.

- 1 cup (120 g) all-purpose flour
- 2 tablespoons (10 g) unsweetened cocoa powder
- 2 tablespoons (25 g) sugar
- $1/2$ teaspoon salt
- $1/4$ cup ($1/2$ stick, or 55 g) unsalted butter
- 2 tablespoons (25 g) solid vegetable shortening
- 1 large egg yolk
- 2 to 3 tablespoons (30 to 45 ml) ice water

1. In a food processor, combine the flour, cocoa, sugar, and salt until blended. Add the butter and shortening and process until the mixture resembles coarse crumbs, about 5 seconds. Add the egg yolk and water and process with on/off turns until the dough forms a ball. (Alternatively, in a medium bowl, mix the flour, cocoa, sugar, and salt. Cut in the butter and shortening with 2 knives or a pastry blender until the mixture resembles coarse crumbs. Add the egg yolk and water and stir with a fork until the mixture begins to clump together.)

2. Press the dough into a ball, then flatten into a 1-inch-thick ($2^1/2$-cm-thick) round. If not using immediately, wrap with plastic and refrigerate for up to 3 days or freeze for up to 3 months.

YIELD: *One 9-inch ($22^1/2$-cm) piecrust*

Charleston Chocolate Pecan Pie

It may not be following the Southern tradition, but adding chocolate to a classic pecan pie vastly improves it, in my humble opinion.

- 4 large eggs
- $^3/_4$ cup (240 g) dark corn syrup
- $^1/_2$ cup (100 g) sugar
- $^1/_4$ cup ($^1/_2$ stick, or 55 g) butter, melted
- 3 tablespoons (45 ml) rum (optional)
- 1 teaspoon (5 ml) vanilla extract
- $^1/_2$ teaspoon salt
- $1^1/_2$ cups (150 g) pecan halves
- 6 ounces (170 g) semisweet chocolate chips
- One 9-inch ($22^1/_2$-cm) unbaked purchased pie shell
- Vanilla ice cream (optional)
- Sweetened whipped cream (optional)

1. Preheat the oven to 350°F (180°C, or gas mark 4). In a large bowl, mix the eggs, corn syrup, sugar, butter, rum (if using), vanilla, and salt.

2. Stir in the pecans and chocolate chips. Pour into the unbaked pie shell. Cover the rim of the pie with aluminum foil.

3. Bake for 25 minutes. Remove the foil and bake for 20 to 25 minutes more, or until the filling is set. Set the pie on a wire rack to cool completely before serving. Serve with vanilla ice cream or whipped cream (or both!), if desired.

YIELD: *8 servings*

Mud Pie

One taste of this rich, dense chocolate pie will send you back for more. It derives its name from the thick mud along the banks of the Mississippi River. During the hot, dry summers, the mud's surface is cracked and dry-looking, much like the top of this pie. But don't let its appearance fool you—a rich, gooey filling lurks just under that crisp surface.

- 1 recipe **Chocolate Pie Pastry** (page 90)
- 2 ounces (55 g) unsweetened chocolate, coarsely chopped
- 1 ounce (30 g) semisweet chocolate, coarsely chopped
- $^1/_2$ cup (1 stick, or 110 g) butter
- 2 teaspoons instant coffee granules or powder
- 3 large eggs
- 1 cup plus 2 tablespoons (225 g) sugar
- $^1/_4$ cup (80 g) light corn syrup
- 1 teaspoon (5 ml) vanilla extract

Americans consumed more than 3.1 billion pounds of chocolate in 2001, which is almost half of the total world's production.

1. Preheat the oven to 350°F (180°C, or gas mark 4). Roll out the dough on a lightly floured surface with a lightly floured rolling pin to form a 12-inch-diameter (30-cm) circle. Line a 9-inch (22^1/$_2$-cm) pie plate with the dough. Trim the edge of the pastry to ^{3}/$_4$-inch (2 cm) wide. Fold the pastry edge under to form a rim. Crimp or flute the rim.

2. Melt the unsweetened and semisweet chocolates with the butter and coffee in the top of a double boiler set over simmering (not boiling) water, stirring until smooth. Remove the pan from the water and let cool slightly. Or put both kinds of the chocolate, the butter, and the coffee into a microwave-safe bowl and microwave on medium for 2 to 4 minutes, until the chocolate is shiny. Remove from the microwave and stir until smooth and melted.

3. In a medium bowl, whisk together the eggs, sugar, corn syrup, and vanilla. Whisk in the chocolate mixture until blended. Pour the filling into the prepared pie crust.

4. Bake until the filling puffs and the top is cracked and slightly crisp, 40 to 45 minutes. Set the pie on a wire rack to cool. (The pie will sink as it cools.) Serve at room temperature.

YIELD: *8 servings*

Sky-High Chocolate Pie

In this classic dessert, a smooth chocolate custard is supported by a dark chocolate crust and topped with snowy mounds of whipped cream. You'll love it, even if it doesn't bring you back to your childhood. It's best eaten on the day it is made.

Chocolate Custard

- 2 cups (475 ml) milk
- 1 cup (235 ml) heavy or whipping cream
- 1/2 cup (100 g) sugar
- 2 large eggs
- 3 tablespoons (25 g) cornstarch
- 7 ounces (170 g) semisweet chocolate, chopped
- 1/4 cup (1/2 stick, or 55 g) butter
- 1 teaspoon (5 ml) vanilla extract

- 1 recipe **Chocolate Pie Pastry** (page 90)

Whipped Cream

- 3/4 cup (175 ml) heavy or whipping cream
- 2 teaspoons (10 g) sugar
- 1/2 teaspoon vanilla extract
- Chocolate shavings, for garnish

To make the custard:

1. In a heavy medium saucepan, heat $1^1/2$ cups of the milk and the cream until tiny bubbles form around the edge. Remove from the heat.

2. In a medium bowl, whisk the remaining $^1/2$ cup of milk with the sugar, eggs, and cornstarch until smooth. Whisk about $^1/2$ cup of the hot milk/cream mixture into the bowl. Repeat with about $^1/2$ cup more of the milk/cream mixture. Pour the contents of the bowl into the saucepan and bring to a boil, whisking constantly. Boil, whisking constantly, for 2 minutes. Remove the pan from the heat and stir in the chocolate, butter, and vanilla, stirring until melted and smooth. Place a sheet of waxed paper or plastic wrap directly onto the surface of the custard to prevent a skin from forming. Refrigerate until thoroughly cooled.

To make the crust:

1. Place the oven rack in the lowest position. Preheat the oven to 425°F (220°C, or gas mark 7). Lightly dust a work surface with cocoa, and roll the dough out to a 13-inch-diameter ($32^1/2$-cm) circle. Line a 9-inch ($22^1/2$-cm) pie plate with the dough. Trim the edge of the pastry to $^3/4$ inch (2 cm) wide. Fold the pastry edge under to form a rim.

2. Line the dough with a double thickness of aluminum foil and bake for 10 minutes. Reduce the oven temperature to 350°F (180°C, or gas mark 4), remove the foil, and bake until the edges are lightly browned, about 10 minutes more. Set the piecrust on a wire rack and cool completely.

continued on next page ➺

To assemble the pie:

1. Pour the custard into the cooled pie shell. Loosely cover and chill for at least 3 hours or up to 12 hours.

2. Just before serving the pie, beat the cream, sugar, and vanilla in a medium bowl with an electric mixer until stiff peaks form when the beaters are lifted. Spread the whipped cream over the pie and decorate with chocolate shavings.

YIELD: *8 to 10 servings*

The superiority of chocolate, both for health and nourishment, will soon give it the same preference over tea and coffee in America which it has in Spain.

THOMAS JEFFERSON

You-Deserve-It Chocolate Cake with Glossy Glaze

This cake is best described as dense, rich, and oh-so-delicious. Almonds add wonderful flavor and texture, but any nuts—hazelnuts or walnuts, for example—can be used. And yes, you deserve every decadent bite!

Cake

- 3 ounces (85 g) bittersweet chocolate, coarsely chopped
- 1 ounce (30 g) unsweetened chocolate
- $3/4$ cup (150 g) sugar
- 10 tablespoons ($1^1/4$ sticks, or 140 g) butter, softened
- 3 large eggs, separated, at room temperature
- 1 teaspoon (5 ml) vanilla extract
- $3/4$ cup (90 g) all-purpose flour
- $1/4$ cup (70 ml) milk
- $2/3$ cup (85 g) ground almonds

Dark Chocolate Glaze

- $1/2$ cup (120 ml) heavy or whipping cream
- 4 ounces (115 g) bittersweet or semisweet chocolate, coarsely chopped

- Sliced almonds, for garnish

continued on next page ➡

To make the cake:

1. Preheat the oven to 350°F (180°C, or gas mark 4). Coat a 9-inch (22^1/$_2$-cm) springform pan with cooking spray, then flour it.

2. Melt the bittersweet and unsweetened chocolates in the top of a double boiler set over simmering (not boiling) water, stirring until smooth. Remove the pan from the water and let cool. Or microwave the chocolate in a microwave-safe bowl or glass measuring cup, uncovered, on medium for 2 to 4 minutes, until shiny (the chocolate won't look melted); remove from the microwave and stir until smooth and melted. Repeat if necessary.

3. Meanwhile, in a large bowl using an electric mixer, beat the sugar and butter until fluffy. Beat in the melted, cooled chocolate, the egg yolks, and the vanilla.

4. With the mixer on low, beat in the flour and milk. Stir in the almonds.

5. In a small bowl, beat the egg whites with clean beaters until stiff peaks form when the beaters are lifted. With a rubber spatula, gently fold the egg whites into the chocolate batter until no streaks of white remain. Spoon the batter into the prepared pan.

6. Bake until the cake springs back when gently pressed and a cake tester inserted into the center comes out clean, 25 to 30 minutes.

7. Set the cake in the pan on a wire rack and cool for 20 minutes. Remove the sides of the pan, turn the cake out onto the rack, and remove the pan bottom. Invert the cake so it is right side up. Let the cake cool completely.

To make the glaze:

1. In a small saucepan, heat the cream over medium heat until small bubbles appear around the edges. Remove the pan from the heat, add the chocolate, and stir until melted and smooth. Let cool to room temperature.

To assemble the cake:

1. Set the cake (still on the rack) over a sheet of waxed paper. Spoon the glaze over the cake and spread it over the top and sides with a large metal spatula. Let stand until the glaze has set.

2. Remove the cake to a serving plate and garnish with sliced almonds.

YIELD: *10 servings*

Once in a while I say, "Go for it" and I eat chocolate.

CLAUDIA SCHIFFER, SUPERMODEL

Chocolate Pudding Cake

If you're not familiar with pudding cakes, then they require faith. You pour hot water over the batter before it goes into the oven. Then it forms a cakelike layer on top of a thick, creamy sauce as it bakes. Serve warm with a spoonful of whipped cream for a true comfort food.

- 3/4 cup (90 g) all-purpose flour
- 2/3 cup (135 g) granulated sugar
- 1/2 cup (45 g) unsweetened cocoa powder
- 1 1/2 teaspoons (7 g) baking powder
- 1/2 teaspoon salt
- 1/2 cup (120 ml) milk
- 3 tablespoons (45 ml) vegetable oil
- 2/3 cup (150 g) packed light brown sugar
- 1/4 cup (45 g) mini semisweet chocolate chips
- 1 teaspoon (5 ml) vanilla extract
- 1 1/4 cups (295 ml) hot water

1. Preheat the oven to 350°F (180°C, or gas mark 4). In an ungreased 8-inch (20-cm) square baking pan, combine the flour, granulated sugar, $1/4$ cup of cocoa, baking powder, and salt. Stir with a fork to mix well. Add the milk and oil. Stir until well blended.

2. Sprinkle the brown sugar, the remaining $1/4$ cup of cocoa, and the chocolate chips over the batter. Mix the vanilla with the water and pour evenly over the top.

3. Bake until the surface looks dry and brownielike, 30 to 35 minutes.

4. Spoon the cake into serving dishes and serve warm or at room temperature.

YIELD: *8 servings*

Wicker baskets filled with cocoa beans were among the gifts the Aztecs offered to the conquistadores.

Nostalgic Chocolate Cupcakes

Who doesn't love cupcakes? Just one bite of these decadent baby cakes will jet you back to the happiest days of your childhood.

Cupcakes

- $3/4$ cup plus 2 tablespoons (75 g) unsweetened cocoa powder
- $1/2$ cup (120 ml) boiling water
- 1 cup (235 ml) buttermilk
- $13/4$ cups (210 g) all-purpose flour
- $11/4$ teaspoons (6 g) baking soda
- $1/4$ teaspoon baking powder
- $1/4$ teaspoon salt
- $3/4$ cup ($11/2$ sticks, or 175 g) unsalted butter, softened
- $11/2$ cups (300 g) sugar
- 2 large eggs, at room temperature
- 1 teaspoon (5 ml) vanilla extract

Icing

- 1 cup (235 ml) heavy or whipping cream
- 8 ounces (225 g) semisweet chocolate, chopped

To make the cake:
1. Preheat the oven to 350°F (180°C, or gas mark 4) and position 2 racks in the lower and middle third of the oven. Line 24 muffin cups with paper or foil liners.

2. Put the cocoa in a medium heat-proof bowl. Add the boiling water and whisk until a smooth paste forms. Whisk in the buttermilk until combined.

3. In a medium bowl, sift the flour with the baking soda, baking powder, and salt.

4. In a large bowl, using an electric mixer, beat the butter with the sugar until light and fluffy, about 3 minutes. Beat in the eggs and vanilla, then beat in the dry ingredients in 2 batches, alternating with the cocoa mixture.

5. Carefully spoon the cupcake batter into the lined muffin cups, filling them about two-thirds full. Bake for 20 to 22 minutes, or until the cupcakes are springy. Let the cupcakes cool in the pans for 5 minutes, then transfer them to wire racks to cool completely.

To make the icing:
1. In a small saucepan, bring the cream to a simmer. Remove the saucepan from the heat and add the semisweet chocolate to the cream. Let stand for 5 minutes, then whisk the melted chocolate into the cream until smooth. Let the chocolate icing stand until slightly cooled and thickened, about 15 minutes.

To assemble the cupcakes:
1. Dip the tops of the cupcakes into the icing, letting the excess drip back into the pan. Transfer the cupcakes to racks and let stand for 5 minutes. Dip the tops of the cupcakes again and transfer them to the racks.

YIELD: *24 cupcakes*

Molten Chocolate Cakes

Warm and oozing with chocolate, these individual-size cakes are satanically tempting. In a contest for "The Most Soothing Food," this would be a serious contender.

- 1^1/$_2$ cups (3 sticks, or 335 g) butter
- ^{3}/$_4$ cup (175 ml) water
- 12 ounces (340 g) semisweet chocolate, chopped
- 1^1/$_2$ cups (300 g) sugar
- 1^1/$_2$ tablespoons (5 g) instant coffee crystals or granules
- Pinch of salt
- 3 tablespoons (45 ml) dark rum
- 1^1/$_2$ tablespoons (25 ml) vanilla extract
- 7 large eggs
- Vanilla ice cream (optional)

1. Preheat the oven to 350°F (180°C, or gas mark 4). Butter six 1¹/₄-cup (295-ml) soufflé dishes or custard cups.

2. In a large saucepan, combine the butter and water and bring to a boil over high heat, stirring until the butter melts. Remove from the heat. Add the chocolate, sugar, coffee, and salt, and stir until the chocolate melts and the mixture is smooth. Stir in the rum and vanilla.

3. In a large bowl, using an electric mixer, beat the eggs to blend, and then gradually beat in the chocolate mixture.

4. Divide the chocolate mixture evenly among the prepared dishes. Bake until the edges of the cakes crack slightly but the center 2 inches (5 cm) remain soft and glossy, about 25 minutes. Serve the cakes warm, topped with vanilla ice cream, if desired.

YIELD: *6 individual-size cakes*

Queen Victoria was such a devotee of chocolate that she sent 500,000 pounds of it to her troops one Christmas.

The Devil's Angel Food Cake

Light and moist, this classic angel food cake is made extra delicious with the addition of cocoa in the batter.

- $^2/_3$ cup (80 g) sifted cake flour
- $^1/_3$ cup (30 g) unsweetened cocoa powder
- $1^1/_2$ cups (300 g) sugar
- 12 large egg whites, at room temperature
- $1^1/_2$ teaspoons ($7^1/_2$ ml) vanilla extract
- $1^1/_2$ teaspoons cream of tartar
- $^1/_2$ teaspoon salt
- $^2/_3$ cup (115 g) mini semisweet chocolate chips
- Cocoa, for dusting (optional)
- Sweetened whipped cream (optional)

Strength is the capacity to break
a chocolate bar into four pieces with your
bare hands——and then eat just one
of the pieces.

JUDITH VIORST, NOVELIST/POET

1. Preheat the oven to 375°F (190°C, or gas mark 5). Sift the flour, cocoa, and 3/4 cup of the sugar together 3 times; set aside.

2. In a large bowl, using an electric mixer, beat the egg whites at low speed until foamy, about 5 minutes. Add the vanilla, cream of tartar, and salt. Gradually increase the speed to medium while beating in the remaining 3/4 cup of sugar, 1 tablespoon at a time, for 5 minutes. When the sugar is blended, continue beating the egg whites until stiff peaks form, about 2 minutes more.

3. Sift one-third of the dry ingredients over the whites; gently fold in with a rubber spatula. Repeat the process 2 more times. Fold in the chocolate chips.

4. Pour the batter into an ungreased 10-inch tube pan. Cut through the batter to remove air pockets. Bake for 40 to 45 minutes, until the top springs back when gently pressed. Turn the pan upside down on a wire rack to cool.

5. To unmold, turn the pan right side up and run a thin knife around the side of the pan and the tube. Re-invert the pan and turn the cake out onto a serving plate. Dust with cocoa and top with whipped cream, if desired.

YIELD: *12 to 14 servings*

Blackout Cake

This cake gets its name not only from its deep, dark color, but also from its effect: One bite may just make you slip into chocolate oblivion! If so, don't forget to return for more.

- 2^1/$_2$ cups (300 g) all-purpose flour
- 1 cup (85 g) unsweetened cocoa powder
- 1 teaspoon baking soda
- ^{1}/$_2$ teaspoon salt
- 1^1/$_2$ cups (3 sticks, or 335 g) unsalted butter, softened
- 3 cups (700 g) granulated sugar
- 5 large eggs
- 2 teaspoons (10 ml) vanilla extract
- 1 cup (230 g) sour cream
- 1 cup (235 ml) boiling water
- Confectioners' sugar, for dusting (optional)

There's more to life than chocolate, but not right now.

ANONYMOUS

1. Preheat the oven to 350°F (180°C, or gas mark 4). Coat a 10-cup Bundt pan with cooking spray, then flour it. In a large bowl, sift the flour with the cocoa, baking soda, and salt.

2. In another large bowl, using an electric mixer, beat the butter until creamy. Add the granulated sugar and beat at medium speed until light and fluffy. Add the eggs, one at a time, beating well after each addition. Beat in the vanilla. At low speed, beat in the dry ingredients in 3 additions, alternating with 3 additions of the sour cream. Gradually beat in the boiling water.

3. Pour the cake batter into the prepared pan. Bake for about 65 minutes, or until a toothpick inserted into the center comes out clean. Let the cake cool in the pan for 5 minutes, then turn out onto a wire rack and let cool completely. Dust lightly with confectioners' sugar, if desired, before slicing and serving.

YIELD: *8 to 10 servings*

Intense Chocolate Loaf

This homespun dessert smells as good while it's baking as it tastes later on. It's best described as a simple cake that lives up to its name. And as they used to say in the old days, "It's a good keeper," meaning it stores well.

- $1/2$ cup (1 stick, or 110 g) butter, softened
- $1^1/4$ cups (250 g) sugar
- $1^1/2$ teaspoons (7 ml) vanilla extract
- 2 large eggs
- 1 cup (85 g) unsweetened cocoa powder
- 1 cup (230 g) sour cream
- $1^3/4$ cups (210 g) all-purpose flour
- 1 teaspoon baking powder
- $1/2$ teaspoon baking soda
- $1/4$ teaspoon salt
- Confectioners' sugar, for dusting

1. Preheat the oven to 350°F (180°C, or gas mark 4). Coat a 9 x 5-inch (22^1/2 x 13-cm) loaf pan with cooking spray, then flour it.

2. In a large bowl, using an electric mixer on medium speed, beat the butter, sugar, and vanilla until light and fluffy, scraping down the sides of the bowl when necessary. Beat in the eggs, one at a time, until well blended.

3. Add the cocoa and sour cream and beat on low speed until blended. Beat in the flour, baking powder, baking soda, and salt.

4. Spoon the batter into the prepared pan. Bake for about 70 minutes, or until a toothpick inserted into the center comes out clean. Transfer the pan to a wire rack and let cool for 20 minutes. Turn the cake out onto the rack and cool completely.

5. Dust with confectioners' sugar before serving.

YIELD: *10 to 12 servings*

The scientific name for the cocoa tree, theobroma cacao, roughly translates to "food of the gods."

Triple Chocolate Cheesecake

The next time your best pal needs some cheering up, this cheesecake should do the trick. You won't find one that is creamier or tastier.

Crust

- 1 box (9 ounces, or 255 g) chocolate wafer cookies
- 7 tablespoons ($^3/_4$ stick, or 85 g) butter, melted

Filling

- 1$^1/_2$ cups (355 ml) heavy or whipping cream
- 1 teaspoon instant coffee powder
- 12 ounces (340 g) semisweet chocolate, finely chopped
- 2 packages (8 ounces, or 225 g, each) cream cheese, at room temperature
- $^3/_4$ cup (150 g) sugar
- 1 tablespoon (10 g) cornstarch
- 1 cup (230 g) sour cream
- 2 teaspoons (10 ml) vanilla extract
- 3 large eggs

Glaze

- $^1/_2$ cup (120 ml) heavy or whipping cream
- 4 ounces (115 g) semisweet chocolate, finely chopped

To make the crust:
1. Preheat the oven to 350°F (180°C, or gas mark 4). Wrap the outside of a 9-inch (22^1/$_2$-cm) springform pan with 2 ^{3}/$_4$-inch-high (7-cm) sides with a double thickness of aluminum foil. Coat the bottom of the pan with cooking spray.

2. In a food processor, finely grind the cookies. Add the butter and process until blended. Press the mixture into the bottom (not the sides) of the prepared pan. Refrigerate while preparing the filling.

To make the filling:
1. In a medium saucepan, combine the cream and coffee powder and stir over medium heat until the coffee powder dissolves. Reduce the heat to low. Add the chocolate and whisk until the chocolate melts and the mixture is smooth. Remove from the heat and let cool for 10 minutes.

2. In a large bowl, using an electric mixer on medium speed, beat the cream cheese and sugar until well blended. Beat in the cornstarch. Add the sour cream and vanilla and beat well. Add the eggs one at a time, beating just until blended after each addition. Whisk 1 cup of the cheese mixture into the chocolate mixture. Return the chocolate mixture to the remaining cheese mixture and whisk until smooth.

3. Pour the batter into the crust. Place the springform pan in a large baking pan. Add enough hot water to the baking pan to come halfway up the sides of the pan. Bake the cheesecake until softly set and slightly puffed around the edges, about 1 hour. Turn off the oven. Let the cake stand in the oven for 45 minutes. Transfer to a wire rack and let cool. Cover and chill the cake in the pan overnight.

continued on next page ➡

To make the glaze:

1. In a heavy small saucepan, bring the cream to a boil. Remove from the heat. Add the chocolate and whisk until melted and smooth. Pour the glaze over the top of the cake. Using a spatula, smooth the glaze evenly over the top. Refrigerate until the glaze is set, at least 2 hours.

2. Using a knife, cut around the sides of the pan to loosen the cake. Remove the pan sides. Cut into wedges and serve.

YIELD: *10 to 12 servings*

What use are cartridges in battle?
I always carry chocolate instead.

GEORGE BERNARD SHAW,
IRISH PLAYWRIGHT AND CRITIC

There were 1,040 U.S. manufacturing establishments producing chocolate and cocoa products in 2001. These establishments employed 45,913 people and shipped $12 billion worth of goods that year. California led the nation in the number of chocolate and cocoa manufacturing establishments (with 116) followed by Pennsylvania (with 107).

Sweet Seduction

CHOCOLATE CAN BE A FOND DECLARATION OF LOVE AND romance, and a plea for its reciprocation—or just a good reason to indulge when you're feeling lonesome and blue. Chocolate is associated with love because eating it can make you feel a similar euphoria.

Chocolate contains a natural "love drug" called phenylethylamine, a chemical that is said to mimic the feeling of being in love by stimulating the brain's pleasure centers. High levels of this neurotransmitter help promote feelings of attraction, excitement, giddiness, and apprehension.

In addition to the "love chemical," chocolate contains more than 500 distinct flavor compounds to perplex and coax the taste buds into paroxysms of delight. No wonder the stuff is so addictive!

The Recipes

Exotic Chocolate Mousse Bars

Sinful Celebration Cake

Chocolate-Raspberry Trifle

Extreme Chocolate Bites

Seductive Soufflé

Warm Chocolate Soufflé Tarts

Brownie Turtle Tart

Venus Truffle Torte

Chocolate Explosion Cake

Chunky Chocolate Gingerbread

Hazelnut Fudge Pie

Double Chocolate Crêpes

Chocolate Muffins

Grilled Dark Chocolate Sandwich

Chocolate Body Paint

Exotic Chocolate Mousse Bars

This totally rich dessert contains chocolate whipped cream between layers of bittersweet chocolate cake topped with a fudgey chocolate glaze. It's best made 1 day ahead and refrigerated overnight.

Cake

- 8 ounces (225 g) bittersweet chocolate, chopped
- 2 teaspoons instant espresso powder dissolved in $^1/_3$ cup (80 ml) hot water
- 6 large eggs, separated
- $^2/_3$ cup (135 g) granulated sugar
- 2 teaspoons (10 ml) vanilla extract
- $^1/_4$ teaspoon cream of tartar
- Pinch of salt
- $^1/_4$ cup (30 g) all-purpose flour
- Unsweetened cocoa powder, for dusting

Filling

- 6 ounces (170 g) bittersweet chocolate, finely chopped
- 2 tablespoons ($^1/_4$ stick, or 30 g) butter
- 2 tablespoons (30 ml) water
- 1$^1/_2$ cups (355 ml) heavy or whipping cream
- 3 tablespoons (20 g) confectioners' sugar
- 1 teaspoon (5 ml) vanilla extract

Glaze

- 1 tablespoon (15 g) solid vegetable shortening
- $^1/_4$ cup (50 g) granulated sugar
- $^1/_3$ cup (80 ml) water
- 4 ounces (115 g) bittersweet chocolate, finely chopped
- 1 ounce (30 g) unsweetened chocolate, finely chopped
- 1 teaspoon (5 ml) vanilla extract

To make the cake:

1. Preheat the oven to 375°F (190°C, or gas mark 5). Coat an 18 x 12-inch (45 x 30-cm) large rimmed baking sheet with cooking spray and line the bottom with parchment or waxed paper. Coat the paper with cooking spray and dust with flour, tapping out any excess.

2. In a small saucepan, combine the chocolate with the dissolved espresso and cook over low heat, stirring constantly, until melted, about 2 minutes. Remove from the heat and let cool slightly.

3. In a medium bowl using an electric mixer, beat the egg yolks at high speed until pale, 2 to 3 minutes. At medium speed, gradually beat in $1/3$ cup (65 g) of the granulated sugar. Increase the speed to high and beat until very thick and pale, about 5 minutes. Add the vanilla and the chocolate mixture and beat at low speed until blended.

4. In a large bowl, using clean beaters, beat the egg whites with the cream of tartar and salt until soft peaks form. Gradually add the remaining $1/3$ cup (65 g) granulated sugar and beat at high speed until the whites are stiff and glossy. Using a large rubber spatula, fold the chocolate mixture and the flour into the whites in 2 batches, until no streaks remain.

5. Spread the batter evenly in the prepared baking sheet. Bake for 12 minutes, or until the cake has risen and is slightly springy. Transfer to a rack and let cool.

continued on next page ➠

6. Run the tip of a knife around the sides of the cake and sift cocoa over the surface. Cover the cake with waxed paper and top with a cutting board. Invert the cake onto the cutting board. Lift off the pan and peel off the paper. Cut the cake in half crosswise, forming 2 rectangles. Chill until firm, about 30 minutes.

To make the filling:
1. In a small saucepan, combine the chocolate with the butter and water. Cook over very low heat, stirring constantly, until melted and shiny. Scrape into a bowl and let cool.

2. Using an electric mixer, beat the cream with the confectioners' sugar and vanilla until firm. Using a rubber spatula, fold in the cooled chocolate.

To make the glaze:
1. In a small saucepan, combine the shortening with the granulated sugar and water and bring to a simmer.

2. Remove the saucepan from the heat, add the bittersweet and unsweetened chocolates, and let stand until melted, about 2 minutes. Whisk in the vanilla. Let the glaze cool until slightly thickened, about 30 minutes.

To assemble the bars:
1. Spread the cream filling over one half of the cake and top with the other half, cocoa side up. Press down lightly and run a cake spatula around the sides to smooth the edges. Pour the glaze down the center of the cake and gently spread it so that it covers the top and drizzles down the sides. Freeze the cake for 4 hours or overnight. Let stand at room temperature until just soft enough to cut. Cut the cake into 3 long strips, then cut each strip into 6 squares. Transfer to plates and serve.

YIELD: *18 bars*

*Forget love. . . I'd rather
fall in chocolate!*

ANONYMOUS

Sinful Celebration Cake

There's always a reason to celebrate—even if it is just to acknowledge the person or people you love. So get over the guilt and indulge with this sensational chocolate tribute to life and love.

Cake

- 4 ounces (115 g) bittersweet or semisweet chocolate, chopped
- 1¹/2 cups (340 g) packed light brown sugar
- ³/4 cup (1¹/2 sticks, or 165 g) unsalted butter, softened
- 4 large eggs
- 1¹/2 cups (180 g) all-purpose flour
- ¹/2 cup (45 g) unsweetened cocoa powder
- 1 teaspoon baking powder
- ¹/2 teaspoon salt
- ¹/4 teaspoon baking soda
- ¹/2 cup (120 ml) whole milk
- ¹/2 cup (125 g) plain yogurt

Buttercream Frosting

- 8 ounces (225 g) bittersweet or semisweet chocolate, chopped
- ¹/2 cup (45 g) unsweetened cocoa powder
- 7 tablespoons (105 ml) water
- 1¹/2 cups (3 sticks, or 335 g) unsalted butter, softened
- 4 cups (400 g) confectioners' sugar
- 1 tablespoon (5 g) grated orange zest
- 2 teaspoons (10 ml) vanilla extract
- ¹/2 teaspoon coarse kosher salt
- Chocolate curls, for garnish

To make the cake:

1. Preheat the oven to 325°F (170°C, or gas mark 3). Coat two 9-inch (22^1/2-cm) round cake pans with cooking spray, then flour them. Line the bottoms of the pans with parchment paper rounds.

2. Stir the chocolate in the top of a double boiler set over simmering (not boiling) water until smooth. Remove the pan from over the water. Cool to barely lukewarm.

3. In a large bowl, using an electric mixer, beat the brown sugar and butter until smooth. Beat in the eggs, one at a time. Beat in the melted chocolate until smooth.

4. In a medium bowl, sift together the flour, cocoa, baking powder, salt, and baking soda.

5. In a small bowl, whisk together the milk and yogurt.

6. Add the dry ingredients, alternating with the milk mixture, in 3 additions each to the chocolate batter. Divide the batter between the prepared pans.

7. Bake the cake for 30 to 40 minutes, or until a cake tester inserted into the centers comes out clean. Cool the cakes in their pans on wire racks for 15 minutes. Turn the cakes out onto the racks; remove the parchment paper and cool completely.

continued on next page ➡➤

To make the frosting:

1. Stir the chocolate in the top of a double boiler set over simmering (not boiling) water until smooth. Cool until barely lukewarm but still pourable.

2. Mix the cocoa and water in a heavy small saucepan. Stir over medium-low heat until smooth and thick but still pourable, adding more water by teaspoonfuls if necessary. Let cool.

3. In a large bowl, using an electric mixer, beat the butter, 1/3 cup (65 g) of the confectioners' sugar, and the orange zest until well blended. Beat in the melted chocolate, vanilla, and salt. Beat in the cocoa mixture. Gradually add the remaining 3 2/3 cups (335 g) of confectioners' sugar and beat until smooth.

To assemble the cake:

1. Place 1 cake layer on a serving platter. Spread 1 1/2 cups (490 g) of the frosting over the top of the cake. Top with the second cake layer. Spread the remaining frosting over the top and sides of the cake, swirling decoratively. Mound chocolate curls in the center of the cake.

YIELD: *10 to 12 servings*

Traditionally, when the cocoa crop was harvested, a dance was performed on the cocoa seeds, which had been put out to dry in the sun. This practice continues today in certain regions of Central and South America.

Chocolate-Raspberry Trifle

One good thing on top of another—chocolatey custard, pound cake, raspberry jam, and fresh whipped cream—describes this dessert that is easy to make and utterly luscious.

Custard

- 1 tablespoon (15 g) sugar
- 1 tablespoon (10 g) cornstarch
- $1/8$ teaspoon salt
- 3 large egg yolks
- 2 cups (475 ml) milk
- 6 ounces (170 g) milk chocolate, chopped

Assembly Ingredients

- 1 cup (235 ml) heavy or whipping cream
- 1 tablespoon (15 g) sugar
- 1 frozen pound cake ($10^3/4$ ounces, or 300 g), package ladyfingers (7 ounces, or 170 g), or angel food cake (9 ounces, or 255 g)
- 2 tablespoons (30 ml) crème de cacao
- $1/4$ cup (80 g) seedless raspberry jam

It's not that chocolates are a substitute for love. Love is a substitute for chocolate. Chocolate is, let's face it, far more reliable than a man.

MIRANDA INGRAM, AUTHOR

To make the custard:

1. In a heavy medium saucepan, mix the sugar, cornstarch, and salt. Whisk in the egg yolks until smooth. Gradually whisk in the milk. Cook over medium heat, stirring constantly, until the custard starts to boil; boil and stir for 1 minute. Remove from the heat and stir in the chocolate until melted and smooth.

2. Transfer to a medium bowl, place plastic wrap directly onto the surface of the custard, and refrigerate until well chilled.

To assemble the trifle:

1. In a medium bowl, using an electric mixer, beat the cream with the sugar until stiff peaks form.

2. Cut the cake into slices $^1/_2$ inch thick ($1^1/_2$ cm). Cut 2 of the cake slices into thin strips and reserve for the top. Arrange about half of the cake slices in the bottom of a 2-quart (2-liter) dessert bowl. Sprinkle with 1 tablespoon (15 ml) of the crème de cacao and spread 2 tablespoons (40 g) of the jam over the cake. Spoon half of the chocolate custard over the cake, then top with half of the whipped cream. Repeat the cake, crème de cacao, jam, and custard layers once. Arrange the reserved cake strips on top of the custard and decorate the top with the remaining whipped cream.

YIELD: *8 to 10 servings*

Extreme Chocolate Bites

They're tiny, they're rich, they're heavenly—and they couldn't be easier to make!

- ◆ ¹/₄ cup (30 g) all-purpose flour
- ◆ ¹/₄ teaspoon baking powder
- ◆ ¹/₈ teaspoon salt
- ◆ 2 large eggs
- ◆ ²/₃ cup (135 g) granulated sugar
- ◆ 1 teaspoon (5 ml) vanilla extract
- ◆ ¹/₂ teaspoon instant espresso powder dissolved in 1¹/₂ teaspoons (7¹/₂ ml) water
- ◆ 5 ounces (140 g) bittersweet chocolate, chopped
- ◆ 2 ounces (55 g) unsweetened chocolate, chopped
- ◆ 2 tablespoons (¹/₄ stick, or 30 g) butter
- ◆ ³/₄ cup (130 g) semisweet chocolate chips
- ◆ Confectioners' sugar (optional)

Chocolate is old-school Viagra.
Montezuma reputedly chugged a cup
of chocolate before entering his harem, while
Casanova called chocolate the "elixir of love"
and drank it instead of champagne.

1. Preheat the oven to 375°F (190°C, or gas mark 5). Line 2 large baking sheets with parchment paper or aluminum foil.

2. In a small bowl, mix together the flour, baking powder, and salt; set aside.

3. Using an electric mixer, beat the eggs, granulated sugar, vanilla, and dissolved espresso in a large bowl until thick and tripled in volume, about 5 minutes.

4. Meanwhile, melt the bittersweet and unsweetened chocolates and the butter in the top of a double boiler set over simmering (not boiling) water, stirring until smooth. Or place in a microwave-safe bowl and microwave on medium (50 percent power) for 1^1/$_2$ to 2 minutes. Stir until the mixture is smooth.

5. Gently fold the chocolate mixture into the egg mixture until just combined. Gently fold in the flour mixture until just combined, then fold in the chocolate chips. Let the batter stand for 15 to 20 minutes to thicken slightly.

6. Drop the batter by heaping teaspoonfuls, 1 inch apart, onto the prepared baking sheets. Bake for 8 to 9 minutes, or until the tops of the cookies are puffed and cracked. Cool completely on the baking sheets. Dust the tops with confectioners' sugar, if desired.

YIELD: *3 dozen cookies*

Seductive Soufflé

There is nothing sexier than sharing a warm chocolate soufflé with your honey. It will transport you both to culinary bliss and is guaranteed to sweeten the night. For a mocha-flavored soufflé, add 1 tablespoon (15 g) of instant coffee powder dissolved in 1 tablespoon (14 ml) of hot water when adding the vanilla to the chocolate mixture.

- 8 ounces (225 g) bittersweet or semisweet chocolate, coarsely chopped
- $^1/_4$ cup ($^1/_2$ stick, or 55 g) butter
- $^1/_8$ teaspoon salt
- $^1/_2$ teaspoon vanilla extract
- 6 large egg yolks
- $^1/_3$ cup (65 g) granulated sugar
- 8 large egg whites
- $^1/_4$ teaspoon cream of tartar
- Confectioners' sugar, for dusting
- Sweetened whipped cream

All I really need is love, but a little chocolate now and then doesn't hurt!

LUCY VAN PELT

(in *Peanuts*, by Charles M. Schulz)

1. Adjust the oven rack to the lower middle position and preheat the oven to 375°F (190°C, or gas mark 5). Butter an 8-cup (1,900-ml) soufflé dish and coat with additional granulated sugar, shaking out any excess sugar; refrigerate until ready to use.

2. Melt the chocolate and butter in the top of a double boiler set over simmering (not boiling) water, stirring until melted and smooth. Turn off the heat, stir in the salt and vanilla, transfer to a large bowl, and set aside.

3. In a medium bowl, using an electric mixer on medium speed, beat the egg yolks and granulated sugar until thick and pale yellow, about 3 minutes. Fold into the chocolate mixture.

4. In another medium bowl, using clean beaters, beat the egg whites until foamy. Add the cream of tartar and beat on high speed until stiff peaks form.

5. Stir one-quarter of the whipped whites into the chocolate mixture. Gently fold the remaining whites into the mixture just until blended.

6. Spoon the mixture into the prepared dish. Bake until the soufflé is set but the interior is still a bit loose and creamy, about 25 minutes. Sift confectioners' sugar over the soufflé and serve immediately with whipped cream.

YIELD: *6 to 8 servings*

Warm Chocolate Soufflé Tarts

These soothing, meltingly rich tarts are one of my favorite desserts. They have just the right blend of textures—crunchy and creamy—and an intriguing, intense flavor. You will need eight individual tartlet pans (4^1/$_2$ by ^{3}/$_4$ inch, or 11^1/$_2$ by 2 cm) with removable bottoms to make them.

Crust

- 1^1/$_2$ cups (180 g) all-purpose flour
- ^{3}/$_4$ cup (1^1/$_2$ sticks, or 165 g) chilled unsalted butter, cut into small pieces
- ^{3}/$_4$ cup (75 g) confectioners' sugar
- ^{1}/$_2$ teaspoon salt

Filling

- 10 ounces (280 g) bittersweet or semisweet chocolate, chopped
- 1^1/$_2$ teaspoons (7 ml) vanilla extract
- 1^1/$_4$ teaspoons (6 g) instant coffee granules or crystals
- Pinch of salt
- 4 large eggs, separated
- ^{1}/$_2$ cup (100 g) granulated sugar
- Sweetened whipped cream, for topping
- Chocolate shavings (optional)

To make the crust:
1. Preheat the oven to 350°F (180°C, or gas mark 4). In a food processor, combine the flour, butter, confectioners' sugar, and salt and process just until the dough gathers together. Shape the dough into a log. Cut into 8 equal rounds.

2. Press 1 round over the bottom and up the sides of each of eight 4^1/$_2$ x 3/4-inch (11^1/$_2$ x 2-cm) tartlet pans with removable bottoms. Pierce the crusts with a fork. Bake the crusts until pale golden, about 18 minutes. Cool in the pans on a wire rack.

To make the filling:
1. Set aside ^{1}/$_3$ cup (60 g) of the chopped chocolate. Place the remaining chopped chocolate in a medium stainless-steel bowl set over a saucepan of barely simmering water (do not allow the bottom of the bowl to touch the water); stir until melted and smooth. Remove the bowl from over the water. Whisk in the vanilla, coffee granules, and salt, then the egg yolks.

2. In another medium bowl, using an electric mixer, beat the egg whites until soft peaks form. Gradually add the granulated sugar, beating until stiff peaks form. Fold half of the whites into the chocolate mixture. Fold in the reserved ^{1}/$_3$ cup (60 g) of chopped chocolate, then the remaining whites. Divide the mixture among the crusts. Freeze for at least 3 hours.

3. Preheat the oven to 375°F (190°C, or gas mark 5). Push the bottom of the frozen tarts up to release them from the pan sides. Arrange the tarts on the pan bottoms on a baking sheet. Bake until the filling puffs and begins to crack, about 20 minutes.

4. Serve the tarts topped with whipped cream and chocolate shavings, if desired.

YIELD: *8 servings*

Brownie Turtle Tart

If you or someone you know loves brownies and caramel, you can enjoy them together in this decadent tart that's rich and chocolatey and sweet and gooey all at the same time.

Chocolate Crust

- $^1/_2$ cup (1 stick, or 110 g) butter, softened
- $^1/_4$ cup (50 g) sugar
- $^3/_4$ cup plus 2 tablespoons (105 g) all-purpose flour
- 2 tablespoons (10 g) unsweetened cocoa powder

Caramel Layer

- $^3/_4$ cup (170 g) individually wrapped caramels (about 17 squares)
- $^1/_4$ cup (60 ml) canned sweetened condensed milk
- $^1/_2$ cup (50 g) pecan pieces, toasted

Brownie Filling

- 2 tablespoons ($^1/_4$ stick, or 30 g) butter
- 2 ounces (55 g) unsweetened chocolate
- 2 large eggs
- $^1/_2$ cup (100 g) sugar
- $^1/_4$ cup (60 ml) canned sweetened condensed milk
- 1 teaspoon (5 ml) vanilla extract

Caramels are only a fad.
Chocolate is a permanent thing.

MILTON S. HERSHEY,
founder of the Hershey Chocolate Company

To make the crust:

1. In a medium bowl, using an electric mixer, beat the butter and sugar until blended and creamy. Beat in the flour and cocoa until blended. Press the mixture over the bottom and up the sides of an 8-inch (20-cm) round tart pan with a removable bottom. Refrigerate for 30 minutes.

To make the caramel layer:

1. Meanwhile, in a small saucepan, combine the caramels and condensed milk and cook over low heat until the caramels melt and the mixture is smooth. Sprinkle the pecans over the bottom of the chilled crust. Pour the caramel mixture over the pecans.

To make the brownie filling:

1. Preheat the oven to 350°F (180°C, or gas mark 4). In a medium saucepan, melt the butter and chocolate over very low heat, stirring often, until smooth.

2. In a medium bowl, using an electric mixer, beat the eggs, sugar, condensed milk, and vanilla until well blended. Stir in the chocolate mixture. Pour over the caramel layer.

3. Bake until the top looks slightly cracked and is no longer shiny, about 45 minutes. Set the tart on a wire rack to cool for 15 minutes before removing the pan sides to cool completely.

YIELD: *8 servings*

Venus Truffle Torte

The serene beauty of this torte makes it an artful ending to a romantic dinner at home.

Torte

- 4 ounces (115 g) semisweet chocolate, chopped
- 1 ounce (30 g) unsweetened chocolate, chopped
- 6 tablespoons ($^3/_4$ stick, or 85 g) butter, softened
- $^1/_3$ cup (65 g) sugar
- 1 teaspoon (5 ml) vanilla extract
- 4 large egg yolks
- 5 large egg whites
- $^1/_4$ teaspoon salt
- 6 tablespoons (50 g) all-purpose flour

Glaze

- 1 cup (175 g) semisweet chocolate chips
- 3 tablespoons (40 g) butter, cut into small pieces
- 1 tablespoon (20 g) light corn syrup

To make the torte:

1. Preheat the oven to 350°F (180°C, or gas mark 4). Coat an 8-inch (20-cm) springform pan with cooking spray, then flour it.

2. In the top of a double boiler, melt the semisweet and unsweetened chocolates over simmering (not boiling) water. Remove the pan from the water and let cool.

3. In a large bowl, using an electric mixer, beat the butter and sugar until light and fluffy. Beat in the vanilla. Beat in the egg yolks, one at a time, until well blended. Beat in the cooled chocolate.

4. In another large bowl, using clean beaters, beat the egg whites and salt until stiff peaks form. Fold the egg whites and the flour alternately into the chocolate mixture until blended.

5. Pour the batter into the prepared pan and spread evenly. Bake for 35 to 40 minutes, or until a toothpick inserted into the center comes out clean. Transfer to a wire rack and let cool for 10 minutes. Remove the side of the pan and let the cake cool completely.

To make the glaze:
1. In the top of a double boiler, melt the chocolate chips with the butter and corn syrup, stirring until smooth. Pour the glaze into a glass measuring cup.

To assemble the torte:
1. Invert the cake onto the rack and remove the pan bottom, then invert the cake right side up.

2. Set the rack over a sheet of waxed paper. Pour the glaze over the cake, letting the glaze drip over the sides. Use a spatula to spread the glaze evenly over the torte. Let it stand for 10 minutes, then transfer it to a serving platter.

YIELD: *8 servings*

Chocolate Explosion Cake

Easy and foolproof, this luscious cake, heaped with dark, rich goodness, is made for every chocolate lover you know. It's worth its weight in chocolate!

- 12 ounces (340 g) bittersweet chocolate, chopped
- $3/4$ cup ($1^1/2$ sticks, or 165 g) unsalted butter, cut into tablespoon-size pieces
- $1^1/2$ teaspoons (10 ml) vanilla extract
- $1/4$ teaspoon plus a pinch of salt
- $3/4$ cup (150 g) sugar
- 5 large eggs, separated and set out at room temperature for 30 minutes
- $1/4$ cup (30 g) all-purpose flour
- Sweetened whipped cream

1. Preheat the oven to 350°F (180°C, or gas mark 4). Coat a 9-inch ($22^1/2$-cm) springform pan with cooking spray and line the bottom with a round of parchment or waxed paper, then coat the paper with cooking spray.

2. Melt the chocolate and butter in a large stainless-steel bowl set over a pan of barely simmering water, stirring frequently. (Or place the chocolate and butter in a large, microwave-safe glass or ceramic bowl and microwave for 4 to 5 minutes, stirring occasionally.) Allow to cool completely. Whisk in the vanilla, $1/4$ teaspoon of salt, and 6 tablespoons (75 g) of the sugar. Add the egg yolks one at a time, whisking well after each addition. Whisk in the flour.

3. In a medium bowl, using an electric mixer, beat the egg whites with a pinch of salt until soft peaks form, then add the remaining 6 tablespoons (75 g) of sugar a little at a time and continue to beat until the whites hold stiff, glossy peaks.

4. Fold about one-fourth of the beaten whites into the chocolate mixture to lighten it, then fold in the remaining whites gently but thoroughly. Pour the batter into the springform pan, spreading it evenly.

5. Bake for 35 to 40 minutes, or until a toothpick inserted into the center comes out with moist crumbs adhering to it.

6. Cool the cake in the pan on a rack for 10 minutes. Remove the side of the pan and cool the cake completely. Invert the cake onto a rack and remove the bottom of the pan, discarding the paper, then invert the cake onto a plate. Serve with whipped cream.

YIELD: *8 servings*

What use are cartridges in battle?
I always carry chocolate instead.

GEORGE BERNARD SHAW,
IRISH PLAYWRIGHT AND CRITIC

Chunky Chocolate Gingerbread

The minute the weather turns the slightest bit cold, our thoughts turn to soothing desserts that warm the heart. Gingerbread is one of those, and it rises to new heights with the addition of chocolate.

- 2¹/4 cups (270 g) all-purpose flour
- 1 tablespoon (5 g) finely chopped crystallized ginger, plus more for garnish (optional)
- 2 teaspoons (5 g) ground cinnamon
- 1 teaspoon baking soda
- 1 teaspoon ground ginger
- ¹/4 teaspoon salt
- ¹/2 cup (1 stick, or 110 g) butter, softened
- ¹/3 cup (65 g) sugar
- 1 large egg
- ³/4 cup (240 g) mild-flavored molasses
- 1 cup (235 ml) brewed coffee, cooled
- 1 cup (175 g) semisweet chocolate chunks
- Sweetened whipped cream (optional)

1. Preheat the oven to 350°F (180°C, or gas mark 4). Coat an 8-inch (20-cm) square baking pan with cooking spray.

2. In a medium bowl, combine the flour, 1 tablespoon of crystallized ginger, cinnamon, baking soda, ground ginger, and salt.

3. In a large bowl, using an electric mixer, beat the butter until smooth. Beat in the sugar until blended. Add the egg and molasses and beat for 1 minute. Alternate adding the dry mixture and coffee to the batter, beating well after each addition. Stir in the chocolate chunks. Pour the batter into the prepared pan.

4. Bake for about 40 minutes, or until a toothpick inserted near the center comes out clean. Cool for 30 minutes in the pan on a wire rack. Serve warm with whipped cream, and sprinkle with additional crystallized ginger, if desired.

YIELD: *6 to 8 servings*

I would give up chocolate,
but I'm no quitter.

ANONYMOUS

Hazelnut Fudge Pie

Snuggle up in bed, turn on a late-night movie, and dig into a wedge of this fudgey pie—it's pure bliss.

- ³/4 cup (170 g) packed light brown sugar
- ¹/4 cup (¹/2 stick, or 55 g) butter, softened
- 3 large eggs
- 12 ounces (340 g) semisweet chocolate chips, melted
- 1 tablespoon (15 ml) dark rum
- ¹/4 cup (30 g) all-purpose flour
- 1 cup (125 g) chopped hazelnuts, toasted
- 1 unbaked 9-inch (22¹/2-cm) pie shell

1. Preheat the oven to 350°F (180°C, or gas mark 4). In a large bowl, using an electric mixer on medium-low speed, beat the brown sugar and butter until well blended. Beat in the eggs, one at a time, until well blended.

2. Add the melted chocolate and rum and beat until blended and smooth.

3. Stir in the flour and hazelnuts.

4. Scrape the filling into the pie shell and spread evenly. Bake until the filling is set and slightly puffed, about 45 minutes. Let cool on a wire rack before serving.

YIELD: *8 servings*

This guy found a bottle in the ocean, and he opened it and out popped a genie, and he gave him three wishes. The guy wished for a million dollars, and poof! There was a million dollars. Then he wished for a convertible, and poof! There was a convertible. And then, he wished he could be irresistible to all women...poof! He turned into a box of chocolates.

ANONYMOUS

Double Chocolate Crêpes

If you're looking for a great dessert or breakfast treat for Valentine's Day, search no further—these delicate, yet decadent, crêpes are just the thing. You can make the crêpes up to 3 days in advance and keep them stacked and wrapped in plastic wrap in the refrigerator.

Crêpes

- 1 cup (120 g) all-purpose flour
- 3 tablespoons (15 g) unsweetened cocoa powder
- 3 tablespoons (40 g) sugar
- $1/2$ teaspoon salt
- $1/2$ cup (120 ml) milk
- 3 large eggs
- 2 tablespoons ($1/4$ stick, or 30 g) unsalted butter, melted and cooled

Filling

- $1/3$ cup (30 g) unsweetened cocoa powder
- $1/3$ cup (65 g) plus 2 tablespoons (25 g) sugar
- $1/4$ cup (30 g) cornstarch
- Pinch of salt
- 1 cup (235 ml) milk
- 1 teaspoon (5 ml) vanilla extract
- 3 large egg whites

- Sweetened whipped cream, for topping
- Unsweetened cocoa powder, for dusting

I never met a chocolate I didn't like.

DEANNA TROI,

(Marina Sirtis) in the TV show *Star Trek: The Next Generation*

To make the crêpes:
1. In a blender or food processor, combine the flour, cocoa, sugar, salt, milk, eggs, and butter and process until well blended.

2. Transfer the batter to a bowl and refrigerate, covered, for 1 hour.

To make the filling:
1. In a medium saucepan, combine the cocoa, $1/3$ cup (65 g) of the sugar, the cornstarch, and the salt. Whisk in the milk. Bring to a boil over medium heat, whisking constantly, until thick and smooth. Remove the pan from the heat, stir in the vanilla, and let the mixture cool.

2. In a medium bowl, using an electric mixer on medium speed, beat the egg whites until soft peaks form. Add the remaining 2 tablespoons (25 g) of sugar, a little at a time, beating until stiff peaks form. Stir one-third of the whites into the cocoa mixture and then fold in the remaining whites gently but thoroughly. Cover and refrigerate until ready to use.

continued on next page ➡➤

To assemble:

1. Coat a nonstick crêpe pan or 6- or 7-inch (15- or 17^1/$_2$-cm) nonstick skillet with cooking spray and heat over medium heat for 30 seconds. Pour ^{1}/$_4$ cup (about 50 ml) of the crêpe batter into the pan, swirling it to coat the bottom of the pan. Cook the crêpe for 1 minute, or until the top appears almost dry. Loosen the edge of the crêpe with a spatula, turn the crêpe, and cook the other side lightly. Transfer the crêpe to a plate. Repeat with the remaining batter in the same manner, lightly greasing the pan as necessary, to make 8 crêpes total.

2. Spread about ^{1}/$_3$ cup (70 g) of the filling in the center of 1 crêpe. Fold 2 sides of the crêpe over the filling. Repeat with the remaining filling and crêpes. Transfer the crêpes to individual serving plates, top with whipped cream, and dust with cocoa. Serve right away.

YIELD: *8 servings*

Chocolate syrup was used for the blood in the famous shower scene in the Alfred Hitchcock movie "Psycho." The scene lasts for about 45 seconds in the movie, but it took 7 days to film.

Chocolate Muffins

These dark gems pack a lot of flavor. The trick to making great muffins is to combine the dry and wet ingredients with a wooden spoon, using as few strokes as possible. Overmixing the batter will give muffins a tough texture.

- 6 tablespoons ($^3/_4$ stick, or 85 g) butter, softened
- 1 cup (235 ml) milk
- 5 ounces (140 g) bittersweet chocolate, chopped
- 2 large eggs
- $1^1/_3$ cups (160 g) all-purpose flour
- $^1/_3$ cup (30 g) unsweetened cocoa powder
- $^1/_3$ cup (75 g) packed light brown sugar
- $1^1/_2$ (7 g) teaspoons baking powder
- $^1/_2$ teaspoon baking soda
- $^1/_2$ teaspoon salt

1. Preheat the oven to 400°F (200°C, or gas mark 6). Coat 12 standard muffin-pan cups with cooking spray or line with paper liners.

2. In a medium saucepan, combine the butter, milk, and half of the chocolate and heat over medium-low heat, stirring until melted and smooth. Remove from the heat and let cool for 15 minutes. Add the eggs and whisk until blended.

3. In a medium bowl, mix the flour, cocoa, brown sugar, baking powder, baking soda, and salt. Add the chocolate mixture and mix just until blended. Stir in the remaining chocolate.

4. Spoon the batter into the prepared cups, dividing evenly. Bake for 14 to 18 minutes, or until a toothpick comes out clean. Cool in the pan on a wire rack for 5 minutes. Remove the muffins to the rack and cool completely.

YIELD: *12 muffins*

Biochemically, love is just like eating large amounts of chocolate.

JOHN MILTON,
the character played by Al Pacino
in the movie, *The Devil's Advocate*

Grilled Dark Chocolate Sandwich

The French have always paired bread with chocolate; consider the chocolate croissant, which is now available everywhere. But this sandwich is both simpler and more decadent

- 4 ounces (115 g) bittersweet chocolate, chopped
- 1/4 cup (60 ml) heavy or whipping cream
- 8 slices plain white bread
- 3 tablespoons (35 g) semisweet chocolate chips
- 3 tablespoons (45 g) butter, softened

1. Put the chocolate into a medium bowl. In a small saucepan, heat the cream just until boiling and pour over the chocolate. Let stand 1 minute, then whisk until smooth. Refrigerate until just slightly solid, about 30 minutes.

2. Spread a layer of the chocolate mixture, about 1/4 inch (1/2 cm) thick (about 2 to 3 tablespoons, or 30 to 40 g), on half of the bread slices to within 1/4 inch (1/2 cm) of the edges. Press about 2 teaspoons (about 10 g) of the chocolate chips into the center of the chocolate spread.

3. Spread 2 tablespoons (30 g) of the softened butter over one side of the remaining bread slices. Buttered-side up, place the slices over each of the chocolate bread slices and press lightly. Refrigerate for 10 minutes.

4. Melt the remaining 1 tablespoon (15 g) of butter in a medium skillet over medium-high heat. Add the sandwiches, and use a spatula to press the unbuttered side down until lightly toasted, about 1 minute. Turn the sandwiches so the buttered side is down and press until the bread is nicely browned, about 1 minute—the chocolate should be barely melted and not running out the sides. Cut in half and serve warm.

YIELD: *4 servings*

Chocolate Body Paint

People have been concocting their own love potions with promises of enhanced virility and increased pleasure for eons. Does it work? Well, everybody has his or her own definition of pleasure, so why don't you see for yourself?

- 2 cups (475 ml) milk
- $2/3$ cup (130 g) sugar
- 2 tablespoons (15 g) cornstarch
- 2 large egg yolks
- $1/2$ teaspoon vanilla extract
- 2 ounces (55 g) unsweetened chocolate, finely chopped
- 1 tablespoon (15 g) butter

1. In a medium saucepan, heat the milk and $1/3$ cup (65 g) of the sugar over medium heat until bubbles appear at the edges.

2. Meanwhile, in a medium bowl, whisk together the remaining $1/3$ cup (65 g) of sugar, cornstarch, egg yolks, and vanilla. Gradually whisk the hot milk into the yolk mixture. Pour the yolk mixture into the saucepan. Cook over medium heat, stirring constantly, until the mixture thickens and comes to a boil; boil for 1 minute.

3. Remove from the heat. Sprinkle the chocolate over the top and let stand for 2 minutes. Whisk in the chocolate and butter until smooth. Pour into a bowl, cover with a sheet of plastic wrap placed directly onto the surface of the body paint, and refrigerate until set.

YIELD: *About 4 cups (900 g)*

Escapism

SPOONFULS OF DARK, RICH, GOOEY CHOCOLATE CAN DO
*a lot more for you than you think—just one bite of a luscious,
decadent dessert can transport you somewhere exotic. And we
know that taking a break from it all is sometimes the best solu-
tion to the doldrums. Nothing invokes the spirit of a culture or
place so much as its cuisine—especially when it's a chocolate
specialty. These international recipes will satisfy your need for
wanderlust without using any of your frequent-flier miles.*

The Recipes

Maui Parfaits

Austrian Chocolate Ring

Rich Chocolate Tiramisu

Chocolate Cannoli

Chocolate-Raspberry Linzer Tart

French Chocolate Pear Cake

Died-and-Went-to-Heaven Crème Brûlée

Chocolate Brioche

Swedish Chocolate Lace Cookies

Bittersweet Brazilian Flan

Chewy Chocolate Macaroons

Mexican Chocolate Cake

Chocolate-Almond-Cherry Stollen

Chocolate Tapas

Chocolate Nachos

Creamy Chocolate-Hazelnut Truffles

Maui Parfaits

Just one spoonful of this magical dessert will transport you to a land where the gods still rule, where a volcano can erupt any minute, where the sun sets every day in a breathtaking crescendo, and where your problems will simply dissolve. Aloha!

- $1/4$ cup (50 g) sugar
- $1^1/2$ tablespoons (10 g) cornstarch
- $1^1/2$ cups (355 ml) whole milk
- 3 large egg yolks
- 4 ounces (115 g) bittersweet or semisweet chocolate, chopped
- 1 teaspoon (5 ml) vanilla extract
- 2 medium ripe bananas
- $1/2$ cup (35 g) shredded coconut, toasted
- $1/2$ cup (65 g) chopped macadamia nuts, toasted

1. In a medium saucepan, whisk together the sugar and cornstarch. Whisk in the milk until well blended, then the egg yolks. Bring to a boil over medium heat. Boil, whisking to keep the milk from sticking to the pan, for 2 minutes or until thickened. Remove from the heat.

2. Sir in the chocolate until melted and smooth, then stir in the vanilla.

3. Pour the mixture into a small bowl and cover with a sheet of plastic wrap placed directly onto the surface of the pudding (to keep a skin from forming). Refrigerate for 1 hour or until chilled.

4. To serve, peel and slice the bananas. Spoon alternating layers of pudding, toasted coconut, bananas, and macadamia nuts into tall dessert glasses.

YIELD: *4 servings*

*Hawaii is the only U.S. state
that grows cocoa beans to produce chocolate.*

Austrian Chocolate Ring

The advantage here is clear: What doesn't get eaten for dessert tonight is perfect for breakfast tomorrow.

Cake

- 1 1/2 cups (180 g) all-purpose flour
- 2 teaspoons baking powder
- 1/4 teaspoon salt
- 1/2 cup (1 stick, or 110 g) butter, softened
- 3/4 cup (150 g) sugar
- 1 teaspoon (5 ml) vanilla extract
- 2 large eggs
- 2/3 cup (155 ml) milk

Filling

- 2 tablespoons (10 g) unsweetened cocoa powder
- 1/4 cup (50 g) sugar
- 1/3 cup (40 g) chopped nuts
- 2 tablespoons (1/4 stick, or 30 g) butter

Great chocolate manufacturers choose their beans in the same way as wine-makers choose their grape varieties.

To make the cake:
1. Preheat the oven to 350°F (180°C, or gas mark 4). Coat a 6- to 7-cup (about 1 1/2-liter) fluted tube pan with cooking spray, then flour it.

2. In a small bowl, mix together the flour, baking powder, and salt.

3. In a large bowl, using an electric mixer, beat the butter with the sugar until light and fluffy. Beat in the vanilla. Beat in the eggs, one at a time, until well blended. Beat in the flour mixture, alternating with the milk, until well blended.

To make the filling:
1. In a small bowl, mix together the cocoa, sugar, and nuts until well blended.

To assemble:
1. Spoon about one-third of the batter into the prepared pan. Sprinkle with half of the filling mixture and dot with 1 tablespoon (15 g) of butter. Spoon over this another one-third of the batter, then the remaining filling mixture and butter. Top with the remaining batter.

2. Bake for 45 to 50 minutes, or until the cake is golden brown and a cake tester inserted into the thickest part comes out clean. Let cool on a wire rack for 10 minutes, then invert and remove the pan and cool completely.

YIELD: *6 to 8 servings*

Rich Chocolate Tiramisu

A favorite Italian dessert, tiramisu means "pick me up." As one story goes, the dessert was created for Venetian courtesans who needed lots of energy for their amorous adventures. There are as many versions of tiramisu as there are cooks in Italy, but this chocolate version is my favorite. Savoiardi are Italian-style ladyfingers sold at Italian import stores, but ordinary ladyfingers found in the supermarket also work well.

Chocolate Zabaglione

- 2 tablespoons (30 ml) heavy or whipping cream
- 1 ounce (30 g) bittersweet or semisweet chocolate, chopped (or $1/4$ cup, or 40 g, chocolate chips)
- 4 large egg yolks
- $1/3$ cup (65 g) sugar
- $1/4$ cup (60 ml) dry Marsala
- Pinch of salt

Assembly Ingredients

- $2/3$ cup (160 ml) heavy or whipping cream
- $1/2$ cup (100 g) sugar
- 6 ounces (170 g) mascarpone cheese
- $2^{1}/2$ cups (595 ml) brewed espresso, warmed
- 32 savoiardi or ladyfingers
- Unsweetened cocoa powder, for garnish
- Dark chocolate, for garnish

To make the zabaglione:

1. In a small saucepan, stir the cream and chocolate over medium heat until the chocolate is melted and the mixture is smooth. Set aside and keep warm.

2. In a large bowl, whisk together the egg yolks, sugar, Marsala, and salt until well blended. Set the bowl over a saucepan of simmering water, but do not allow the bottom of the bowl to touch the water. Whisk the egg mixture over the simmering water until it is thick and creamy, about 4 minutes. Remove from the heat.

3. Fold the chocolate mixture into the egg mixture. Cover and refrigerate until completely chilled.

To assemble:

1. In a medium bowl, using an electric mixer, beat the cream and $1/4$ cup (50 g) of the sugar until soft peaks form.

2. Put the mascarpone into a large bowl and fold in the whipped cream, then fold in the chilled zabaglione. Cover and refrigerate.

3. In a small bowl, whisk together the espresso and the remaining $1/4$ cup (50 g) of sugar. Line a $9^1/4$ x 5 x $2^3/4$-inch (23 x 13 x 7-cm) stainless-steel loaf pan with plastic wrap, allowing the plastic to extend over the sides. Dip 8 savoiardi into the espresso and arrange them in a single layer side by side over the bottom of the prepared pan.

continued on next page ➡→

4. Spoon one-third of the mascarpone mixture over the cookies to cover. Repeat the dipping of 8 of the cookies into the espresso and layering the cookies and remaining mascarpone mixture two more times. Dip the remaining 8 cookies into the espresso and arrange side by side atop the tiramisu. Press lightly to compact slightly (the last layer will extend above the pan sides). Cover the tiramisu with plastic wrap and refrigerate for at least 6 hours.

5. Unwrap and invert the tiramisu onto a serving platter. Remove the plastic wrap. Sift the cocoa over the tiramisu. With a vegetable peeler or sharp knife, make dark chocolate shavings and sprinkle over the top.

YIELD: *10 to 12 servings*

*Venice is like eating an entire
box of chocolate liqueurs in one go.*

TRUMAN CAPOTE,
AMERICAN NOVELIST/SHORT STORY WRITER

Chocolate Cannoli

Crisp-fried cannoli shells are available at Italian food import shops. Fill them with this creamy chocolate-ricotta mixture, and then sit back and watch them quickly disappear.

- 1 cup (175 g) milk chocolate chips
- 1 container (15 ounces, or 425 g) ricotta cheese
- 2 packages (3 ounces, or 85 g, each) cream cheese
- 2 tablespoons (15 g) confectioners' sugar
- 1 teaspoon (5 ml) vanilla extract
- 12 prepared 5-inch (13-cm) cannoli shells
- 1/3 cup (40 g) finely chopped nuts

1. In the top of a double boiler, melt the chocolate chips over simmering (not boiling) water, stirring until smooth. Remove from the water and let cool to room temperature.

2. In a medium bowl, using an electric mixer, beat the ricotta until smooth. Add the cream cheese, sugar, and vanilla and beat well. Beat in the cooled melted chocolate.

3. Spoon the mixture into the cannoli shells. Dip the ends into the nuts. Chill until ready to serve.

YIELD: *12 cannoli*

Chocolate-Raspberry Linzer Tart

I don't know whether the Germans or the Austrians deserve credit for coming up with the sensational flavor combination of chocolate, raspberry, and almonds, but they both use these ingredients to great advantage in numerous desserts. Here is one irresistible example.

- 3/4 cup (1 1/2 sticks, or 165 g) butter
- 1/2 cup (100 g) granulated sugar
- 2 large egg yolks
- 1/2 teaspoon baking powder
- 1/4 teaspoon ground cinnamon
- 1/8 teaspoon ground cloves
- 1/8 teaspoon salt
- 1 cup (120 g) all-purpose flour
- 1 cup (125 g) finely ground almonds
- 3 ounces (85 g) semisweet chocolate, finely ground in a food processor
- 2/3 cup (215 g) seedless raspberry jam
- Confectioners' sugar, for dusting

Nine out of ten people like chocolate.
The tenth person always lies.

JOHN Q. TULLIUS,
ARTIST/CARTOONIST

1. Coat a 9-inch (22^1/2-cm) springform pan with cooking spray. In a medium bowl, using an electric mixer, beat the butter and granulated sugar until light and fluffy. Beat in the egg yolks, baking powder, cinnamon, cloves, and salt until blended.

2. In a small bowl, mix the flour and almonds. Add to the butter mixture and beat just until blended. Beat in the chocolate.

3. With lightly floured fingers, press approximately 1^1/2 cups (approximately 195 g) of the batter over the bottom of the prepared pan. Spoon the jam over the batter and spread evenly, leaving a ^{1}/2-inch (1^1/2-cm) border around the edge.

4. Spoon the remaining batter into a large pastry bag fitted with a large round plain tip. Pipe the batter in a lattice pattern over the preserves. Or, with the palms of your hands, roll out thin logs of dough 9 inches (22^1/2 cm) long using about 1 tablespoon (about 10 g) of dough for each one. Arrange the dough pieces in a lattice pattern over the filling. Chill the tart for 30 minutes.

5. Preheat the oven to 350°F (180°C, or gas mark 4). Bake the tart until the jam begins to bubble and the crust is firm and lightly golden, about 50 minutes. Set the tart in the pan on a wire rack to cool.

6. To serve, remove the sides of the pan and transfer the tart to a serving plate. Dust with confectioners' sugar.

YIELD: *8 servings*

French Chocolate Pear Cake

In France, pears are often matched with chocolate in spectacular desserts such as this cake. A glass of Sauternes or sweet muscatel wine would complement the cake nicely.

- 1 cup (120 g) all-purpose flour
- 3 tablespoons (15 g) unsweetened cocoa powder
- 1/2 teaspoon baking powder
- 3 ripe Bartlett pears (about 1 1/2 pounds, or 680 g), peeled and cored
- 2/3 cup (135 g) plus 1 tablespoon (15 g) granulated sugar
- 1/2 cup (1 stick, or 110 g) butter, softened
- 2 large eggs
- 2 ounces (55 g) semisweet chocolate, chopped
- Confectioners' sugar, for garnish

1. Preheat the oven to 350°F (180°C, or gas mark 4). Coat a 9-inch (22 1/2-cm) springform pan with cooking spray, then flour it.

2. In a small bowl, combine the flour, cocoa, and baking powder.

3. Cut each pear lengthwise into quarters, then cut each quarter lengthwise in half.

4. In a large bowl, using an electric mixer on medium speed, beat $^2/_3$ cup (135 g) of the granulated sugar and the butter until light and fluffy. Beat in the eggs, one at a time, until blended. On low speed, beat in the flour mixture just until blended. Stir in the chocolate.

5. Spread $1^1/_2$ cups (about 180 g) of the batter into the prepared pan. Arrange the pear slices with the tapered ends toward the center, overlapping them around the edge of the pan (do not cover the center with fruit). Sprinkle the pears with the remaining 1 tablespoon (15 g) of granulated sugar. Spread the top with the remaining batter (it will not cover the fruit completely).

6. Bake for 30 to 35 minutes, or until a toothpick inserted into the center of the cake comes out clean. Cool the cake in the pan on a wire rack. Remove the side of the pan and sift confectioners' sugar over the top of the cake. Serve warm or at room temperature.

YIELD: *6 to 8 servings*

Marie Antoinette had a personal chocolatier from Vienna, who devised such concoctions as chocolate mixed with powdered orchid bulbs, which was thought to pleasingly plump out the figure.

Died-and-Went-to-Heaven Crème Brûlée

Few desserts are more luxurious than a chocolate crème brûlée. Rich, smooth, and decadent with a thin, crisp, caramelized sugar topping—it's the stuff your chocolate dreams are made of.

- 1$^{1}/_{2}$ cups (355 ml) heavy or whipping cream
- $^{1}/_{2}$ cup plus 2 tablespoons (150 ml) milk
- 3$^{1}/_{2}$ ounces (100 g) bittersweet chocolate, finely chopped
- 5 large egg yolks
- $^{1}/_{3}$ cup plus 1 teaspoon (70 g) granulated sugar
- $^{1}/_{4}$ cup (55 g) packed light brown sugar

1. Preheat the oven to 300°F (150°C, or gas mark 2). In a medium saucepan, bring the cream and milk to a boil over medium heat. Remove from the heat, stir in the chocolate, and let it stand until melted, about 5 minutes.

2. In a medium bowl, whisk the egg yolks with the granulated sugar until blended. Whisk in the chocolate mixture. Strain the custard into a large measuring cup, and then pour it into six 4-ounce (120-ml) ramekins.

3. Set the ramekins in a baking dish and add enough hot water to the dish to reach halfway up the sides of the ramekins. Bake for about 40 minutes, or until the custards are set. Remove from the water bath and let cool. Cover and refrigerate for at least 6 hours or overnight.

4. Preheat the broiler. Sprinkle the brown sugar evenly over the custards and broil as close to the heat as possible for about 20 seconds, or until the sugar melts. Serve right away.

YIELD: *6 servings*

As with most fine things, chocolate has its season. There is a simple memory aid that you can use to determine whether it is the correct time to order chocolate dishes: Any month whose name contains the letter A, E, or U is the proper time for chocolate.

SANDRA BOYNTON, AUTHOR
Chocolate: The Consuming Passion

Chocolate Brioche

Brioche is a traditional buttery, rich bread sold throughout France in neighborhood pastry shops and sidewalk cafés. A slice of this delectable chocolate version is great lightly toasted for breakfast or an afternoon snack.

- 1 package ($^1/_4$ ounce, or 7 g) active dry yeast
- 6 tablespoons (90 ml) warm water (105° to 115°F, or 41° to 46°C)
- 2$^3/_4$ cups (330 g) all-purpose flour
- 2 tablespoons (25 g) sugar
- 1 teaspoon salt
- 6 tablespoons ($^3/_4$ stick, or 85 g) butter, softened
- 6 tablespoons (90 ml) heavy or whipping cream
- 4 large egg yolks
- $^2/_3$ cup (115 g) semisweet chocolate chips
- 1 large egg, beaten

1. Coat an 8-inch (20-cm) brioche mold with cooking spray. In a small bowl, dissolve the yeast in the warm water and let stand for 10 minutes, or until foamy.

2. Add $^3/_4$ cup (90 g) of the flour and stir until smooth. Cover with plastic wrap and let the mixture rise in a warm, draft-free place for 1 hour.

3. In a large bowl, combine the remaining 2 cups (240 g) of flour, the sugar, and the salt. Make a well in the center and add the yeast mixture, butter, cream, and egg yolks, mixing until a dough forms. Turn the dough out onto a lightly floured surface and knead until it's smooth and elastic, about 5 minutes. Knead in the chocolate chips.

4. Reserve one-fourth of the dough. Form the remaining dough into a ball and place in the prepared pan. Make a deep depression in the center of the dough. Roll the reserved dough into a ball. Press it into the center of the dough in the pan. Pat the topknot to shape it evenly. Cover with plastic wrap coated with cooking spray and let rise in a warm place until doubled in volume, about 1 hour.

5. Preheat the oven to 350°F (180°C, or gas mark 4). Brush the beaten egg gently over the brioche. Bake for 40 minutes, cover lightly with aluminum foil, and bake for an additional 15 minutes. Remove the brioche from the pan and set on a wire rack to cool slightly. Serve warm.

YIELD: *4 to 6 servings*

If one swallows a cup of chocolate only 3 hours after a copious lunch, everything will be perfectly digested and there will still be room for dinner.

ANTHELME BRILLAT-SAVARIN (1755–1826)

wrote La Physiologie du Gout *or*
The Physiology of Taste, *first translated in 1925.*

Swedish Chocolate Lace Cookies

This recipe yields thin, chocolate nut wafers that are brittle and lacy. Drizzled with a chocolate glaze, they look fancy and taste yummy.

Cookies

- 3 ounces (85 g) German sweet chocolate, coarsely chopped
- 1 1/2 tablespoons (25 ml) milk
- 6 tablespoons (3/4 stick, or 85 g) butter, softened
- 1/2 cup (115 g) packed light brown sugar
- 1 teaspoon (5 ml) vanilla extract
- 1/4 cup (30 g) all-purpose flour
- 1/4 teaspoon baking soda
- 1 cup (75 g) quick oats
- 1/2 cup (65 g) finely chopped pecans, toasted

Glaze

- 1 ounce (30 g) German sweet chocolate
- 1/2 teaspoon vegetable oil

Mozart wrote about chocolate! He made reference to chocolate in his opera Cosi Fan Tutte.

To make the cookies:
1. Preheat the oven to 350°F (180°C, or gas mark 4). Line several baking sheets with parchment paper. In a small saucepan, melt the chocolate with the milk over medium-low heat, stirring until smooth. Set aside.

2. In a large bowl, beat the butter and brown sugar with a mixer on high speed until light and fluffy. On low speed, beat in the chocolate mixture and vanilla until blended. Beat in the flour and baking soda until blended. Stir in the oats and pecans.

3. Drop the batter by rounded teaspoonfuls 3 inches (7^1/2 cm) apart onto the prepared sheets.

4. Bake for 10 minutes, or until the cookies spread and have a lacy appearance. Lift the parchment off the baking sheets, transfer to wire racks, and cool completely.

5. Carefully peel the cookies from the paper and set onto a sheet of waxed paper.

To make the glaze:
1. In the top of a double boiler set over simmering (not boiling) water, melt the chocolate with the oil, stirring until smooth. Using a fork, drizzle the glaze back and forth over the cookies in a random pattern. Let them stand until the glaze is set, about 30 minutes.

YIELD: *3^1/2 dozen cookies*

Bittersweet Brazilian Flan

Smooth and rich, with a slightly bitter caramel taste, this flan is a wonderful make-ahead dessert because it needs to chill overnight.

- 1^3/$_4$ cups (350 g) sugar
- 2 tablespoons (30 ml) fresh lemon juice
- 4 cups (950 ml) milk
- 6 ounces (170 g) bittersweet or semisweet chocolate, coarsely chopped
- 8 large eggs
- ^{1}/$_2$ teaspoon vanilla extract
- ^{1}/$_4$ teaspoon cinnamon

Seventy percent of the world's chocolate comes from just three places: the Ivory Coast, Ghana, and Indonesia.

1. Preheat the oven to 300°F (150°C, or gas mark 2). In a heavy medium saucepan, combine 1 cup (200 g) of the sugar with the lemon juice. Stir with a wooden spoon over medium heat until the sugar melts, then cook, stirring occasionally, until the sugar turns deep brown, about 10 minutes. Pour the hot caramel into an 8-cup (2-liter) metal ring mold; carefully tilt the mold to coat the interior with the caramel. If needed, use a wooden spoon to push the caramel up the sides.

2. In another heavy medium saucepan, combine the milk with the remaining $3/4$ cup (150 g) of sugar. Cook over medium heat, stirring occasionally, until the sugar dissolves. Add the chocolate, cover, and remove the pan from the heat. Set aside until the chocolate is melted, then stir well.

3. In a medium bowl, lightly beat the eggs. Gradually whisk in the hot milk, vanilla, and cinnamon until well blended.

4. Strain the custard into a large glass measuring cup, and then pour it into the ring mold. Cover the flan loosely with aluminum foil and set the mold in a baking dish or roasting pan. Pour enough hot water into the baking dish to reach halfway up the side of the mold. Bake in the center of the oven for about 70 minutes, or until the flan is set but still jiggly in the center.

5. Remove the mold from the baking dish. Let the flan cool to room temperature, then refrigerate overnight. Run a small sharp knife around the side of the mold, cover with a large rimmed plate, and invert the mold onto the plate. Cut the flan into wedges and serve.

YIELD: *12 servings*

Chewy Chocolate Macaroons

For a wallop of chocolate and coconut—and who doesn't love that combination?—try these delectable, chewy cookies. Your kids will love them, as will your Saturday-night guests.

- 2 bags (7 ounces, or 195 g, each) sweetened shredded coconut
- 1 1/4 cups (220 g) mini semisweet chocolate chips
- 1/3 cup plus 1 tablespoon (50 g) all-purpose flour
- 1/4 teaspoon salt
- 3/4 cup (95 g) finely chopped pecans, toasted
- 1 can (14 ounces, or 396 g) sweetened condensed milk
- 2 teaspoons (10 ml) vanilla extract

1. Preheat the oven to 350°F (180°C, or gas mark 4). Lightly coat 2 large baking sheets with cooking spray.

2. In a large bowl, combine the coconut, chocolate chips, flour, salt, and pecans. Add the condensed milk and vanilla and stir until blended.

3. Spoon level tablespoonfuls of the batter onto the prepared baking sheets. Bake for about 20 minutes, or until lightly golden but still moist inside. Set on a wire rack to cool completely.

YIELD: *4 dozen cookies*

After about 20 years of marriage, I'm finally starting to scratch the surface of what women want. And I think the answer lies somewhere between conversation and chocolate.

MEL GIBSON, ACTOR/DIRECTOR

Mexican Chocolate Cake

Cinnamon adds an intriguing flavor to this humbly named but very sophisticated cake.

Cake

- 1 cup (2 sticks, or 225 g) unsalted butter
- 1/2 cup (45 g) unsweetened cocoa powder
- 3/4 cup (175 ml) water
- 2 cups (400 g) granulated sugar
- 2 large eggs
- 1/2 cup (120 ml) buttermilk
- 2 tablespoons (30 ml) vanilla extract
- 2 cups (240 g) all-purpose flour
- 1 teaspoon baking soda
- 1/2 teaspoon cinnamon
- 1/4 teaspoon salt

Glaze

- 1/4 cup (1/2 stick, or 55 g) butter
- 1/2 cup (120 ml) half-and-half
- 1/2 cup (50 g) confectioners' sugar
- 5 ounces (140 g) bittersweet chocolate, finely chopped
- 2 cups (250 g) chopped pecans, toasted
- 1/4 teaspoon salt

To make the cake:
1. Preheat the oven to 350°F (180°C, or gas mark 4). Coat a 9-inch (22^1/$_2$-cm) tube pan or 12-cup (3-liter) Bundt pan with cooking spray. Flour the pan, shaking out any excess flour.

2. In a large saucepan, melt the butter over medium-low heat. Whisk in the cocoa. Add the water and whisk until smooth. Remove from the heat. Whisk in the granulated sugar, eggs, buttermilk, and vanilla until well blended.

3. In a medium bowl, sift together the flour, baking soda, cinnamon, and salt. Add to the cocoa mixture and whisk until just combined.

4. Pour the batter into the prepared cake pan and bake for 45 to 55 minutes, or until a toothpick or cake tester inserted into the thickest part comes out with a few moist crumbs. Cool the cake on a wire rack for 20 minutes, then loosen the edges with a thin knife and invert onto a plate.

To make the glaze:
1. In a medium saucepan, melt the butter over low heat. Stir in the half-and-half and confectioners' sugar. Add the chocolate and cook, stirring, until smooth. Remove from the heat and stir in the pecans and salt. Let the glaze cool until slightly thickened, about 5 minutes.

2. Spoon the glaze over the top and sides of the cake and spread with a small offset spatula or knife to cover completely.

YIELD: *10 to 12 servings*

Chocolate-Almond-Cherry Stollen

This rich stollen is special-occasion bread in Germany, where it is served with whipped butter or toasted for breakfast.

Stollen

- 2^1/2 to 3 cups (300 to 360 g) all-purpose flour
- 2 packages (^{1}/2 ounce, or 14 g, total) active dry yeast
- ^{2}/3 cup (160 ml) milk
- ^{1}/4 cup (50 g) granulated sugar
- 2 tablespoons (^{1}/4 stick, or 30 g) butter
- ^{1}/2 teaspoon salt
- 1 large egg
- 1 cup (175 g) semisweet chocolate chips
- ^{1}/3 cup (50 g) dried cherries
- ^{1}/3 cup (40 g) chopped almonds, toasted
- Egg wash: 1 egg yolk beaten with 1 teaspoon (5 ml) water

Glaze

- ^{1}/2 cup (50 g) confectioners' sugar
- ^{1}/2 teaspoon vanilla extract
- 2 teaspoons (10 ml) milk

To make the stollen:
1. In a large bowl, combine 1 cup (120 g) of the flour and the yeast. In a small saucepan, combine the milk, granulated sugar, butter, and salt. Cook over medium-low heat, stirring often, until the butter is melted. Add to the flour mixture and stir until smooth.

2. Add the egg and mix well. Stir in the chocolate chips, cherries, and almonds and as much of the remaining flour as can be mixed into the dough.

3. Turn the dough out onto a lightly floured surface and knead in enough of the remaining flour to make a moderately stiff dough that is smooth and elastic, kneading for about 5 minutes. Divide the dough into thirds, cover with a clean kitchen towel, and let rest for 10 minutes.

4. Roll each dough third into a "rope" 18 inches (45 cm) long. Braid the three "ropes" together loosely, beginning in the middle and working toward each end. Press the ends to seal and tuck under. Place the bread on a baking sheet, cover with plastic wrap coated with cooking spray, and let rise in a warm spot until doubled in volume, about 1 hour.

5. Preheat the oven to 350°F (180°C, or gas mark 4). Brush the bread with the egg wash. Bake the stollen for 30 to 35 minutes, or until golden brown.

To make the glaze:
1. In a small bowl, mix together the confectioners' sugar, vanilla, and milk. (Add more milk if necessary to make the mixture the desired consistency; it should be thin enough to pour, but not runny.) Drizzle the glaze over the cooled bread.

YIELD: *16 slices*

Chocolate Tapas

In the Catalonia region of Spain, no party would be complete without a bread-based tapas such as this indulgent treat. It's a sure crowd-pleaser.

- 10 baguette slices, $^1/_2$-inch ($1^1/_2$-cm) thick
- 3 to 4 tablespoons (45 to 60 ml) extra virgin olive oil
- 3 ounces (85 g) bittersweet or semisweet chocolate, finely chopped

1. Preheat the broiler. Place the bread slices on a baking sheet and broil until toasted, about 5 minutes.

2. Reduce the oven temperature to 350°F (180°C, or gas mark 4). Drizzle each baguette slice with oil. Sprinkle each slice with some of the chopped chocolate.

3. Bake for 5 minutes, or until the chocolate is melted. Serve warm.

YIELD: *4 to 5 servings*

Las cosas claras y el chocolate espeso.
(Ideas should be clear and chocolate thick.)

SPANISH PROVERB

Chocolate Nachos

These may not be your traditional nachos, but I bet you won't be able to eat just one.

- ¹/₄ cup (50 g) sugar
- ¹/₄ teaspoon ground cinnamon
- 8 (6-inch, or 15-cm) flour tortillas
- ¹/₄ cup (¹/₂ stick, or 55 g) butter, melted
- 1 cup (175 g) semisweet chocolate chips
- 2 teaspoons (10 g) solid vegetable shortening

1. Preheat the oven to 350°F (180°C, or gas mark 4). In a small bowl, mix the sugar and cinnamon. Brush one side of each tortilla with melted butter; sprinkle with the sugar mixture. Cut each tortilla into 8 wedges.

2. Arrange the wedges in a single layer on 2 baking sheets. Bake for 10 to 12 minutes, or until the edges are lightly browned.

3. Meanwhile, in a small saucepan, melt the chocolate chips with the shortening, stirring until melted and smooth.

4. Remove the tortilla wedges from the oven. Arrange the tortillas in an even layer on a large serving platter and let cool slightly. Drizzle with the melted chocolate mixture. Serve warm or cool.

YIELD: *8 servings*

Creamy Chocolate-Hazelnut Truffles

Luxurious and expensive, truffles are the European aristocrats of chocolate. But this recipe proves that you don't have to travel abroad to enjoy them at their finest.

The better the chocolate you use, the better these truffles will be—and they are incredibly easy to make.

- 8 ounces (225 g) bittersweet or semisweet chocolate, chopped
- $^1/_2$ cup plus 2 tablespoons (150 ml) heavy or whipping cream
- 1 tablespoon (15 ml) brandy
- $^1/_4$ teaspoon vanilla extract
- 6 tablespoons (45 g) ground hazelnuts, toasted
- $1^1/_2$ cups (190 g) chopped hazelnuts, toasted

The higher the quality of the chocolate, the louder it should snap when you break it.

1. Put the chocolate into a medium bowl. In a small saucepan, bring the cream to a simmer. Pour the cream over the chocolate and let stand for 2 minutes. Whisk until smooth. Mix in the brandy and vanilla. Cool completely, stirring occasionally, for about 30 minutes.

2. Using an electric mixer, beat the chocolate mixture until fluffy and lighter in color, about 4 minutes. Mix in the ground hazelnuts. Cover and refrigerate the mixture until firm, about 2 hours.

3. Line a baking sheet with waxed paper. Place the chopped hazelnuts in a medium bowl. Fill a measuring cup with hot water. Dip a 1-inch-diameter ($2^1/2$-cm) melon baller into the water, then into the truffle mixture, forming a round truffle. Drop the truffle into the nuts and roll to coat it completely; press to make the nuts adhere. Place on the prepared sheet. Repeat with the remaining truffle mixture and nuts. Cover and chill until firm, about 1 hour.

YIELD: *3 to 4 dozen truffles*

Surrender to Savory

IF YOU ARE FEELING DEPLETED AND WANT TO GET
happy, retreat to your kitchen and try cooking up some chocolate
in a savory dish. Don't scoff at the notion of making dinner out
of chocolate. Rich, dark chocolate is not only for desserts, but for
spicy and savory dishes as well.

The Spanish, Italians, and Mexicans have long known that
chocolate adds a luxurious texture and intriguing flavor to
savory foods. And thanks to an ever-growing supply of high-
quality chocolate from around the world, as well as new products such as cocoa nibs, more and more chefs and cooks are
exploring the not-so-sweet side of chocolate. Just one taste of
chili with a hint of chocolate, or cocoa-and spice-rubbed flank
steak, or chocolate-infused meat sauce ladled over pasta will
convert you to a savory chocolate fan.

The Recipes

Pan-Roasted Chicken with Mole Sauce

Grilled Steak with Cocoa Spice Rub

Chili with Chocolate

Sweet and Spicy Chicken Stew

Pasta Bolognese with Chocolate

Chocolate-Chicken Enchiladas

Grilled Shrimp with Cocoa Romesco Sauce

Braised Short Ribs with Chocolate

Chocolate Vinaigrette

Chocolate Oatmeal

Chocolate Bread

Pan-Roasted Chicken with Mole Sauce

There are many mole sauces in Mexico, but to me the best is the one with chocolate added. This is an easy, streamlined version of the classic. Tomatillos are pale green fruit (rather like green cherry tomatoes in size and shape) with a distinctive lemon flavor. They help tone down the spiciness of the sauce. The mole sauce can be made ahead and refrigerated in an airtight container for up to 1 week.

Mole Sauce

- 2 cups (475 ml) boiling water
- 5 dried ancho chiles, rinsed, with seeds removed
- $1/4$ cup (60 ml) dry sherry
- $1/3$ cup (40 g) raisins
- 6 small fresh tomatillos, husks removed
- 1 pound (455 g) plum tomatoes, halved lengthwise
- 2 corn tortillas
- $1/4$ cup (55 g) shelled raw pumpkin seeds
- $1/2$ teaspoon ground cinnamon
- $1/4$ teaspoon ground cloves
- 1 can (14$1/2$ ounces, or 410 g) chicken broth
- 2 teaspoons (10 ml) vegetable oil
- 1 medium onion, chopped
- 2 teaspoons (5 g) minced garlic
- $1/4$ cup (40 g) whole almonds
- 1 teaspoon salt
- 2 ounces (55 g) unsweetened chocolate, chopped

Chicken

+ 1 tablespoon (15 g) butter

+ 1 tablespoon (15 ml) olive oil

+ 1 chicken (4 pounds, or approximately 2 kg),
  cut into 8 pieces

+ Salt and freshly ground black pepper

To make the mole sauce:

1. In a medium bowl, pour the boiling water over the chiles.

2. In a small saucepan, heat the sherry. Add the raisins, remove from the heat, and let stand for 20 minutes to plump.

3. Meanwhile, preheat the broiler. Arrange the tomatillos and tomatoes cut sides down on a rimmed baking sheet. Lightly coat with cooking spray and broil for 12 to 14 minutes, or until the skins are evenly charred. Let cool, then peel the tomatoes and transfer with the tomatillos to a blender.

4. Heat a heavy griddle or skillet over medium heat. Toast the tortillas for 2 to 3 minutes, or until lightly browned on both sides. Tear into small pieces and set aside.

5. In a medium skillet, toast the pumpkin seeds until they pop, about 2 minutes. Add to the roasted tomatoes and tomatillos in the blender. Add the cinnamon and cloves to the skillet and toast, stirring, for 30 seconds to 1 minute, or just until fragrant. Transfer to the blender.

continued on next page ➡➤

6. Puree the mixture in the blender until smooth, adding about $1/2$ cup (120 ml) of the chicken broth. Pour into a large saucepan or Dutch oven.

7. Heat the oil in the same skillet. Add the onion and cook over medium heat, stirring often, for 3 minutes. Add the garlic and almonds and cook, stirring often, for 2 minutes more. Transfer to the blender. Add the soaked chilies and their liquid, the raisins and sherry, and the tortillas, and puree until smooth. Add to the saucepan with the roasted tomato mixture, the remaining $10 1/2$ ounces of broth, and the salt. Bring to a boil, reduce the heat, and simmer, partially covered, stirring occasionally, for 30 minutes. Stir in the chocolate until melted.

To make the chicken:
1. Meanwhile, heat the oven to 450°F (230°C, or gas mark 8). In a large ovenproof skillet, melt the butter with the oil over medium heat. Season the chicken with salt and pepper. Add the chicken to the skillet and cook, turning occasionally, until browned, about 10 minutes. Transfer the skillet to the oven and roast for about 20 minutes, or until the chicken is cooked through. Serve hot with the mole sauce.

YIELD: *4 servings*

The cocoa tree can be found only within 10 degrees latitude of the equator. It grows no more than 250 feet above sea level and needs rich soil and lots of moisture and shade to thrive.

Grilled Steak with Cocoa Spice Rub

This unique spice rub will add deep flavor not only to beef, but to pork, chicken, and lamb as well. Any extra rub will keep in an airtight container for up to 3 months.

- 2 tablespoons (15 g) ground cinnamon
- 2 tablespoons (10 g) unsweetened cocoa powder
- 1 tablespoon (20 g) sea salt
- 1 teaspoon grated nutmeg
- 1 teaspoon ground coriander
- 1 teaspoon freshly ground white pepper
- $1/2$ teaspoon ground cloves
- 1 pound (455 g) flank steak, trimmed

1. In a small bowl, mix the cinnamon, cocoa, salt, nutmeg, coriander, pepper, and cloves. Rub the spice mixture on both sides of the steak.

2. Prepare a grill to medium-high heat. Grill the steak on an oiled rack set 5 to 6 inches (13 to 15 cm) over the coals for 6 to 8 minutes on each side (for medium-rare meat). Transfer the steak to a cutting board and let it stand for 10 minutes. Holding a sharp knife at a 45-degree angle, cut the steak across the grain into very thin slices.

YIELD: *4 servings*

Chili with Chocolate

Don't tell your friends that you added chocolate to their favorite chili dish—let them guess what the subtle, rich flavor is. Use any leftovers to make tacos, Mexican salads, or nachos, or use as a baked-potato topping.

- 1 tablespoon (15 ml) vegetable oil
- 2 large onions, chopped (2 cups, or 260 g)
- 3 garlic cloves, minced
- 2 pounds (910 g) lean ground beef
- 1 can (15 ounces, or 425 g) tomato sauce
- 1 cup (235 ml) beef broth
- 2 tablespoons (20 g) chili powder
- 2 tablespoons (20 g) semisweet chocolate chips
- 2 tablespoons (30 ml) vinegar
- 2 tablespoons (40 g) honey
- 1 tablespoon (10 g) pumpkin pie spice
- 1 teaspoon ground cumin
- $1/2$ teaspoon ground cardamom
- $1/4$ teaspoon ground cloves
- 2 cans (15 ounces, or 425 g, each) kidney beans
- 3 cups (12 ounces, or 340 g) shredded Cheddar cheese

1. In a large Dutch oven, heat the oil over medium heat. Add the onions and garlic and cook, stirring often, until softened, about 8 minutes. Add the beef and cook, stirring often, until browned, about 8 minutes. Drain off the fat.

2. Stir in the tomato sauce, beef broth, chili powder, chocolate chips, vinegar, honey, pumpkin pie spice, cumin, cardamom, cloves, and kidney beans. Bring to a simmer, cover, reduce the heat, and simmer for 1 hour.

3. Skim off the fat. Spoon the chili into serving bowls. Top each with some cheese and serve hot.

YIELD: *8 servings*

You should bait mousetraps with chocolate, not cheese. European researchers found that mice are more attracted to cocoa than to Cheddar.

Sweet and Spicy Chicken Stew

Cracked black pepper adds spiciness to this one-pot meal that balances well with the rich flavor of the chocolate and the sweetness of the butternut squash and apple. Serve this amazingly flavorful stew over couscous or with mashed potatoes.

- 1 tablespoon (15 ml) olive oil
- 1 large red bell pepper, seeded and coarsely chopped ($1^1/2$ cups, or 180 g)
- 1 large red onion, cut into thin wedges
- 2 medium tart apples, such as Granny Smith, cored and chopped
- 4 skinless, boneless chicken breast halves (about 1 pound, or 455 g), cut into bite-size pieces
- 2 small zucchini, sliced into $1/2$-inch-thick ($1^1/2$-cm) rounds
- 1 tablespoon (10 g) minced fresh garlic
- $2^1/2$ cups (570 ml) chicken broth
- 2 tablespoons (10 g) chopped fresh thyme or 1 teaspoon dried
- 2 teaspoons (4 g) coarsely ground black pepper
- $1/2$ teaspoon salt
- 1 package (20 ounces, or 570 g) frozen butternut squash chunks
- $1/2$ ounce (15 g) bittersweet or semisweet chocolate, grated

1. In a large pot, heat the oil over medium heat. Add the bell pepper and onion and cook, stirring occasionally, for 4 to 5 minutes, or until the onion is softened.

2. Add the apples, chicken, zucchini, garlic, chicken broth, thyme, pepper, and salt to the pot. Bring to a boil.

3. Reduce the heat to low, cover, and simmer for 8 to 10 minutes, stirring occasionally, until the zucchini is crisp-tender.

4. Stir in the butternut squash. Return to a boil. Reduce the heat to low. Cover and simmer for 5 to 7 minutes, or until the vegetables are tender and the chicken is cooked through. Stir in the chocolate until melted and smooth. Serve warm.

YIELD: *4 servings*

In 1980, news of chocolate espionage stunned the world when an apprentice of Suchard-Tobler (the Swiss company that produces Toblerone) unsuccessfully attempted to sell secret chocolate recipes to Russia, China, Saudi Arabia, and other countries.

Pasta Bolognese with Chocolate

This dish, a specialty of northern Italy's Emilia-Romagna region, is named for the region's capital city. Chocolate imparts a complementary undertone to the meaty sauce. It is classically paired with tagliatelle (ribbon pasta just slightly wider than fettuccine), but it also goes well with a variety of pasta shapes that trap the savory sauce.

- 2 tablespoons (30 ml) olive oil
- 2 tablespoons (^{1}/4 stick, or 30 g) butter
- 1 small onion, finely chopped
- 1 medium carrot, finely chopped
- 1 medium celery rib, finely chopped
- ^{1}/2 pound (225 g) lean ground chuck
- ^{1}/2 pound (225 g) ground pork
- Salt and black pepper
- 1 cup (235 ml) milk
- Freshly grated nutmeg
- 1 cup (235 ml) dry white wine
- 1 can (28 to 32 ounces, or 825 to 940 ml) whole tomatoes with juice
- 2 ounces (55 g) unsweetened chocolate, chopped
- 1 pound (455 g) dried pasta, such as tagliatelle, penne, rigatoni, fusilli, or orecchiette

1. In a heavy large saucepan, heat the oil and butter over medium-high heat. Add the onion, carrot, and celery, and cook, stirring often, until the vegetables begin to soften, about 4 minutes. Add the beef and pork, and cook, stirring often, for 5 minutes, or until the meat is no longer pink. Season with salt and pepper to taste.

2. Add the milk and the nutmeg to taste, and cook, stirring often, until most of the milk has evaporated, about 10 minutes. Add the wine and cook, stirring occasionally, until the liquid has evaporated, about 10 minutes.

3. In a blender or food processor, coarsely puree the tomatoes with their juice and stir into the sauce. Simmer the sauce, uncovered, stirring occasionally, for 75 minutes (the sauce will thicken).

4. Stir in the chocolate until melted and smooth and season with additional salt and pepper.

5. Bring a large pot of lightly salted water to a boil. Add the pasta, stirring to prevent sticking, and cook according to the package directions or until al dente, about 10 minutes. Drain in a colander. In a large heated bowl, immediately toss the pasta with the sauce and serve.

YIELD: *6 servings*

Chocolate-Chicken Enchiladas

Enchiladas are a great example of how Mexican cooks are gifted at coaxing full flavors out of humble ingredients. The addition of chocolate to the sauce adds a distinctive flavor and aroma. These are easy to make and will be a hit with adults as well as kids.

- 8 (8-inch, or 20-cm) flour tortillas
- 1¹/2 cups (165 g) chopped cooked chicken or turkey
- 1 can (11 ounces, or 310 g) whole-kernel corn with sweet peppers, drained
- ¹/3 cup (80 g) lowfat cream cheese
- ¹/4 cup (60 g) lowfat dairy sour cream
- ¹/4 cup (25 g) sliced green onions
- 2¹/2 cups (330 g) cut-up fresh tomatillos
- 1 can (4 ounces, or 115 g) chopped green chiles, drained
- ¹/4 cup (35 g) chopped onion
- ¹/4 cup (15 g) chopped cilantro
- ¹/2 teaspoon sugar
- ¹/4 teaspoon ground cumin
- 1¹/2 cups (355 ml) chicken broth
- 1 ounce (30 g) bittersweet or semisweet chocolate, chopped
- ³/4 cup (85 g) shredded Monterey Jack cheese

1. Preheat the oven to 350°F (180°C, or gas mark 4). Coat a 3-quart (3-liter) rectangular baking dish with cooking spray.

2. Stack the tortillas and wrap them tightly in aluminum foil. Bake the tortillas for 10 minutes to soften.

3. In a medium bowl, combine the chicken, corn, cream cheese, sour cream, and green onions. Spoon about $1/3$ cup (about 65 g) of this filling onto each tortilla near an edge; roll up. Arrange the filled tortillas, seam sides down, in the prepared baking dish.

4. In a blender or food processor, combine the tomatillos, chiles, onion, cilantro, sugar, and cumin. Add the chicken broth and process until smooth. Transfer the mixture to a saucepan. Bring to a boil, reduce the heat, and simmer, uncovered, for 10 minutes. Stir in the chocolate until melted and smooth.

5. Pour the sauce over the enchiladas. Cover with aluminum foil and bake for about 45 minutes, or until heated through. Remove the foil, sprinkle with the Monterey Jack, and bake for 5 minutes more, or until the cheese is melted. Serve hot.

YIELD: *4 servings*

In the United States, the retail chocolate industry generates $13 billion per year.

Grilled Shrimp
with Cocoa Romesco Sauce

This classic sauce is from the Catalonia region of Spain. Here it's embellished with cocoa nibs, small pieces of husked roasted cocoa beans that are available in gourmet food shops. They have all the earthy flavor of eating chocolate without the sweetness. If you can't find the nibs, unsweetened chocolate will work here, too.

Cocoa Romesco Sauce

- 1 medium tomato, halved crosswise and seeded
- 1 small red bell pepper
- $^1/_4$ cup plus 2 tablespoons (90 ml) extra virgin olive oil
- 3 tablespoons (25 g) sliced almonds
- 1 garlic clove, minced
- 1 teaspoon crushed red pepper
- 3 tablespoons (20 g) coarse dry bread crumbs
- 2 tablespoons (15 g) cocoa nibs or unsweetened chocolate, grated
- 2 tablespoons (30 ml) sherry vinegar
- Salt and freshly ground black pepper

Shrimp

- 2 pounds (905 g) large shrimp, shelled and deveined
- Vegetable oil, for brushing
- Salt and freshly ground black pepper

To make the cocoa romesco sauce:

1. Preheat the broiler. Place the tomato and bell pepper in a baking dish and broil until the skins are charred. Transfer the pepper to a bowl, cover with plastic wrap, and let steam for 5 minutes. Peel the vegetables and discard the charred skins, seeds, and stems. Coarsely chop the tomato and pepper, and place them in a food processor along with any accumulated juices.

2. In a small skillet, heat the oil. Add the almonds and cook over moderate heat, stirring, until slightly golden, about 3 minutes. Add the garlic and crushed red pepper and cook for 1 minute. Stir in the bread crumbs and remove from the heat. Scrape the mixture into the food processor. Add the cocoa nibs and vinegar and process until almost smooth. Scrape the sauce into a bowl and season with salt and pepper to taste.

To make the shrimp:

1. Prepare a grill or heat a lightly oiled grill pan. Brush the shrimp with vegetable oil and season with salt and pepper to taste. Grill the shrimp 5 to 6 inches (13 to 15 cm) above the coals for 1 minute per side, or until lightly charred and just cooked through. Alternatively, cook the shrimp in the grill pan over high heat for 1 to 2 minutes per side. Serve the hot shrimp with the sauce alongside for dipping.

YIELD: *6 servings*

Braised Short Ribs with Chocolate

These succulent ribs are braised in a gravy made dark and rich with a bit of chocolate. They are even better the next day.

- 6 pounds (about 3 kg) beef short ribs, cut into 1-rib pieces
- Salt and freshly ground black pepper
- 1 tablespoon (15 ml) olive oil
- 3 medium onions, chopped
- 4 large garlic cloves, minced
- 1^1/$_2$ cups (355 ml) dry red wine
- 1 can (28 to 32 ounces, or 825 to 940 ml) whole tomatoes, including liquid, coarsely pureed in a blender
- 1^1/$_2$ cups (355 ml) beef broth
- 2 tablespoons (30 ml) Worcestershire sauce
- 2 teaspoons grated orange zest
- 2 teaspoons chopped fresh rosemary leaves or 1 teaspoon dried
- ^{1}/$_2$ teaspoon salt
- 2 cups (420 g) pearl onions, blanched in boiling water for 2 minutes and peeled
- 6 medium carrots, peeled and cut into 1^1/$_2$-inch (4-cm) pieces
- 2 ounces (55 g) bittersweet or semisweet chocolate, finely chopped

The fruit of the cacao tree grows directly from the trunk. The fruits look like small melons, and the pulp inside contains 20 to 50 seeds, or beans. It takes about 400 beans to make a pound of chocolate.

1. Pat the short ribs dry and season them with salt and pepper to taste. In a heavy large Dutch oven, heat the oil over medium-high heat. Brown the ribs in batches, transferring them with tongs to a large bowl. Set the browned ribs aside.

2. Add the chopped onions to the pot and cook over medium heat, stirring often, until golden. Add the garlic and cook, stirring, for 1 minute. Add the wine, tomatoes, beef broth, Worcestershire sauce, orange zest, rosemary, and salt and bring to a boil. Add the ribs, including any juices that have accumulated in the bowl. Reduce the heat, cover, and simmer for 30 minutes.

3. Add the pearl onions and carrots, stirring and pushing them down to make sure they are covered by liquid, and simmer, covered, for 60 to 90 minutes, or until the meat is tender. Transfer the meat, pearl onions, and carrots with a slotted spoon to a large bowl.

4. Bring the braising liquid to a boil and boil, stirring occasionally, until slightly thickened and reduced to about 5 cups (about 1,100 ml). Stir in the chocolate until melted and smooth. Return the meat and vegetables to the pot and cook over low heat, stirring occasionally, until heated through. Serve hot.

YIELD: *6 servings*

Chocolate Vinaigrette

There are many uses for this uniquely flavored vinaigrette. It's great as a salad dressing, for deglazing pans for gravies and sauces, and drizzled over fruit or cheese.

- $1/2$ (scant) cup (100 g) sugar
- 3 tablespoons (45 ml) apple cider vinegar
- 3 tablespoons (45 ml) balsamic vinegar
- 1 ounce (30 g) bittersweet or semisweet chocolate, grated

1. In a small saucepan, combine the sugar and the apple cider and balsamic vinegars. Cook over medium heat, stirring often, until the sugar has dissolved. Pour the mixture into a small bowl. Add the chocolate, let stand for 1 minute, then whisk until melted and smooth. Let cool to room temperature.

YIELD: *3/4 cup (175 ml)*

There are Cocoa Exchanges
in New York, London, Hamburg, and
Amsterdam. Market price depends on the
abundance of the worldwide crop, the quality
of the beans, and economic conditions
throughout the world.

Because chocolate is such a high-energy food, Sir Edmund Hillary brought it with him on his expedition to the top of Mt. Everest.

Chocolate Oatmeal

Start the day out right with a bowl of warm, creamy oatmeal. Its goodness reaches new heights of comfort when chocolate is added. This recipe can easily be doubled to serve four.

- $1^1/3$ cups (315 ml) vanilla soymilk
- $2/3$ cup (50 g) quick-cooking Irish oatmeal
- $1/2$ ounce (15 g) bittersweet or semisweet chocolate, grated
- Light brown sugar, for sprinkling

1. In a heavy medium saucepan, combine the soymilk and oatmeal. Cook over medium heat, stirring often, until the mixture comes to a simmer and thickens, about 4 minutes.

2. Remove the pan from the heat, add the chocolate, and stir until it's melted and smooth. Spoon the oatmeal into serving bowls and sprinkle with brown sugar.

YIELD: *2 servings*

Chocolate Bread

This sweet yeast bread is bursting with the flavor of chocolate. It's a good example of the magical effect chocolate has on a food.

Bread

- 1 package ($^1/_4$ ounce, or 7 g) active dry yeast
- $^1/_2$ cup (120 ml) warm water (105° to 110°F, or 41° to 43°C)
- 2$^3/_4$ cups (330 g) all-purpose flour
- $^1/_3$ cup (30 g) unsweetened cocoa powder, preferably Dutch processed
- 3 tablespoons (40 g) granulated sugar
- 1 teaspoon salt
- $^1/_2$ teaspoon ground cinnamon
- 2 tablespoons ($^1/_4$ stick, or 30 g) unsalted butter, cut into small pieces
- $^1/_4$ cup (60 ml) milk
- 1 large egg
- 2 ounces (55 g) bittersweet or semisweet chocolate, finely chopped

Icing

- 2 cups (200 g) confectioners' sugar
- 3 tablespoons (45 ml) water
- 1 tablespoon (15 g) unsalted butter
- 1 tablespoon (20 g) light corn syrup
- 1 teaspoon (5 ml) vanilla extract

- $1/4$ to $1/3$ cup (30 to 40 g) slivered or sliced almonds, toasted

To make the bread:

1. In a small bowl, mix together the yeast and water; let stand until foamy, about 5 minutes.

2. In a large bowl, combine the flour, cocoa, granulated sugar, salt, and cinnamon, and stir to blend. Add the butter, milk, egg, chocolate, and yeast mixture. Using an electric mixer, beat on low speed until the dough is smooth, about 5 minutes.

3. Coat a bowl with cooking spray. Transfer the dough to the bowl and turn to coat. Cover with plastic wrap coated with cooking spray and let rise in a warm place until doubled in size, about 1 hour.

continued on next page ➡

4. Punch down the dough and turn it out onto a lightly floured surface. Knead briefly. Divide the dough into 3 equal pieces and roll each under the palms of your hands into a 16-inch-long (40-cm) rope. Place the 3 ropes side by side on a large baking sheet coated with cooking spray. Starting at one end, braid the ropes together, being careful not to overstretch the dough. Pinch the ends of the braid and tuck under to seal.

5. Cover with plastic wrap coated with cooking spray and let rise until almost doubled, about 1 hour.

6. Preheat the oven to 350°F (180°C, or gas mark 4). Bake the bread until it's firm to the touch, about 40 minutes. Transfer the bread to a wire rack to cool.

To make the icing:
1. In a medium saucepan, combine the confectioners' sugar, water, butter, corn syrup, and vanilla. Place over low heat and stir constantly for 2 to 3 minutes, until the mixture is warm and has the consistency of heavy cream. Drizzle the icing over the braided loaf and decorate the top with the almonds.

YIELD: *16 servings*

Christopher Columbus was the first
European to discover cocoa beans upon landing
in Nicaragua on his fourth voyage, in 1502.
However, he and his entourage, who were
still searching for a sea route to India,
showed little interest in them.

The Chocolate Glossary

Alkalized cocoa powder

Cocoa powder that has been treated with an alkali during processing to neutralize the natural acidity of the chocolate and produce a darker-colored, milder-tasting cocoa. This cocoa can be labeled as "alkalized," "treated with an alkali," or "Dutch processed."

Baking chocolate

Unsweetened or bitter chocolate.

Bittersweet chocolate

Chocolate liquor sweetened with sugar and blended with cocoa butter, lecithin (an emulsifier), and flavorings such as vanilla or vanillin. Bittersweet chocolate, also called dark chocolate, must be at least 35 percent chocolate liquor. It can be used interchangeably with semisweet chocolate.

Cacao

The cacao tree grows in South and Central America, Africa, Southeast Asia, and the West Indies. It is cultivated for its seed pods, which are used to produce chocolate.

Chocolate bloom

When chocolate develops either powdery-looking white blotches or grainy, rough surfaces, it is called chocolate bloom. Bloom is a sign that the chocolate has not been properly stored. The first case, fat bloom, is caused by warmth, and the second, sugar bloom, is caused by dampness. Bloom is not harmful, and when the chocolate is melted, it disappears.

Chocolate extract

This extract looks like vanilla extract, but it has a decidedly chocolate flavor. Use it when you want to add an extra dose of chocolate flavor to a dessert. Use it in addition to vanilla extract or to replace up to half the amount of vanilla extract called for in chocolate dessert recipes.

Chocolate liquor

Pure unsweetened chocolate liquid produced by grinding the cocoa nibs. It contains approximately 50 percent cocoa butter. When hardened, chocolate liquor becomes unsweetened or bitter chocolate.

Cocoa butter

Fat naturally occurring in the cocoa bean that is first extracted and then returned to the chocolate in varying amounts, depending on the manufacturing and the type of chocolate produced.

Cocoa nibs

Tiny pieces of roasted, cracked cocoa beans that have not yet been ground into chocolate liquor. They have no sugar added, so they are pure, unadulterated chocolate. They taste like unsweetened chocolate with a dry, crunchy texture. Cocoa nibs can be added to a variety of chocolate desserts for extra texture and an extra layer of flavor.

Conching

Rolling chocolate between heavy rollers to refine it and develop flavor while ingredients such as sugar and milk solids are added. The length of conching affects the chocolate's texture.

Couverture

Dark chocolate with a high percentage of cocoa butter (from 32 to 39 percent) used for coating, hand-dipping, and molding, because it melts so smoothly and forms a thin, shiny shell.

Dark chocolate

Sweetened chocolate liquor with milk solids. Also called bitter-sweet and semisweet chocolate.

Dutch-processed cocoa powder

Alkalized cocoa powder.

Ganache

A mixture of melted dark chocolate and heavy cream, which, depending on its temperature and consistency, is formed into truffles or used as a frosting, filling, or sauce.

Lecithin

A natural substance (a member of the phospholipid family) that emulsifies fats. Chocolate manufacturers use it to emulsify, or smooth out, the chocolate.

Milk chocolate

Chocolate containing milk solids, sugar, cocoa butter, and flavorings such as vanilla and vanillin. Milk chocolate made in the United States usually contains 10 percent chocolate liquor and 12 percent whole milk.

Nonalkalized cocoa powder

Cocoa powder that has not been treated with an alkali. It has a lighter color and a stronger chocolate flavor than alkalized cocoa powder. Also called natural cocoa powder.

Pistoles

Pronounced "pih STOHLZ," pistoles are flat wafers or disks of chocolate. Some chocolate manufacturers are making their chocolate available in this form so it is easier to use, because it saves you from having to chop large bars or chunks of chocolate into small pieces. Pistoles can be melted easily, just like chopped chocolate, in a double boiler or a microwave oven.

Seizing

When chocolate lumps and hardens. This occurs when water or moisture mistakenly comes in contact with melted chocolate.

Semisweet chocolate

Chocolate liquor sweetened with sugar and blended with cocoa butter, lecithin (an emulsifier), and flavorings such as vanilla or vanillin. Semisweet chocolate must be at least 35 percent chocolate liquor (the specific percentage varies by manufacturer) and therefore is often exactly the same in composition as bittersweet chocolate. The two can be used interchangeably. Also called dark chocolate.

Sweet chocolate

Chocolate that is 15 percent chocolate liquor and blended with sugar, cocoa butter, milk solids, and flavorings. Also called German Sweet Chocolate, after a man named Sam German who first produced the chocolate in a factory near Boston in 1852. Cannot be substituted for dark chocolate.

Tempered chocolate
When the cocoa butter crystals are stable. Tempered chocolate is necessary for candy-making, enrobing (coating), and molding. Chocolate is in temper when it leaves the manufacturer. When melted, chocolate is out of temper.

Unsweetened chocolate
Baking or bitter chocolate.

White chocolate
This type of chocolate is made from cocoa butter, sugar, milk solids, lecithin, and flavorings, and contains no chocolate liquor. It gets its mild chocolate flavor from the cocoa butter.

Index

SUBJECT INDEX

RECIPE INDEX

A

almonds
Change-Your-World Tartufo, 66–67
Chocolate-Almond-Cherry Stollen, 178–179
Chocolate Clementines, 38
Chocolate-Raspberry Linzer Tart, 162–163
Grilled Shrimp with Cocoa Romesco Sauce, 198–199
Pan-Roasted Chicken with Mole Sauce, 186–188
You-Deserve-It Chocolate Cake with Glossy Glaze, 97–99

apples
Sweet and Spicy Chicken Stew, 192–193

apricots
Forever Fondue, 32–33
Austrian Chocolate Ring, 156–157

B

bananas
Forever Fondue, 32–33
Maui Parfaits, 54–155
Stressless Smoothie, 46

beef
Braised Short Ribs with Chocolate, 200–201
Chili with Chocolate, 190–191
Grilled Steak with Cocoa Spice Rub, 189
Pasta Bolognese with Chocolate, 194–195

bell peppers
Grilled Shrimp with Cocoa Romesco Sauce, 198–199
Sweet and Spicy Chicken Stew, 192–193

beverages
Chocolate Martini, 42
Double Chocolate Mochaccino, 45
Shameless Chocolate Shake, 71
Sisterhood Shake, 39
Stressless Smoothie, 46
Thick Mudslide, 43
Wickedly Good Hot Chocolate, 40

bittersweet chocolate
Bittersweet Brazilian Flan, 172–173
Braised Short Ribs with Chocolate, 200–201
Change-Your-World Tartufo, 66–67
Chocolate Bread, 204–206

Chocolate-Chicken Enchiladas, 196–197
Chocolate Clementines, 38
Chocolate Decadence Ice Cream Pie, 56–57
Chocolate Explosion Cake, 138–139
Chocolate Muffins, 148–149
Chocolate Oatmeal, 203
Chocolate Tapas, 180
Chocolate Vinaigrette, 202
Creamy Chocolate-Hazelnut Truffles, 182–183
Dark and Delicious Pear Sundaes, 50–51
Devil's Food Pancakes, 34–35
Died-and-Went-to-Heaven Crème Brûlée, 166
Exotic Chocolate Mousse Bars, 118–120
Extreme Chocolate Bites, 128–129
Forever Fondue, 32–33
Grilled Dark Chocolate Sandwich, 150
Heavenly Bittersweet Rice Pudding, 85
Killer Brownies, 76–77
Maui Parfaits, 154–155
Mexican Chocolate Cake, 176–177
Outrageous Warm Chocolate Pudding, 88–89
Rich Chocolate Tiramisu, 158–160
Seductive Soufflé, 130–131
Sinful Celebration Cake, 122–124
Sweet and Spicy Chicken Stew, 192–193
Warm Chocolate Soufflé Tarts, 132–134
Wickedly Good Hot Chocolate, 40
You-Deserve-It Chocolate Cake with Glossy Glaze, 97–99

Bittersweet Granita, 70

Black-and-White Ice Cream Sandwiches, 62–63

Blackout Cake, 108–109

body paint, 151

Braised Short Ribs with Chocolate, 200–201

bread, as ingredient
Chocolate Bread Pudding, 86–87
Chocolate Tapas, 180
Grilled Dark Chocolate Sandwich, 150

bread recipe
Chocolate Bread, 204–206

brioche
Chocolate Brioche, 168–169

brownies
Brownie Turtle Tart, 134–135
Killer Brownies, 76–77